Walking in Bristol

by

HELENA EASON

Maps by Catherine Leendertz

KINGSMEAD

Kingsmead Press
Rosewell House
Kingsmead Square
Bath

SBN 901571 85 7

Text set in 10/11 pt Photon Baskerville, printed by photo-lithography, and bound in Great Britain at The Pitman Press, Bath

INTRODUCTION

John Betjeman regarded Bristol as, "still the most beautiful, interesting and distinguished city in England", and much of the charm of the city lies in its succession of well defined areas, each having its own group of fine buildings, churches and centres of interest.

The aim of this book is to help you to explore the city in a series of walks which will take you in turn to these centres of interest and give you a complete picture of the history of Bristol. If you are a visitor and only have time, literally, to walk around the area, then you will still get a good overall impression of the importance of the city from these walks. If, however, you are a Bristolian who really wants to know the city in which you live, why not give a half, or even a whole day to each walk and examine all the places mentioned in detail? You could take the children on a series of walks in the school holidays and let them learn about their heritage in an easy but organised way. There is something in each walk to see, to do, to examine and to admire.

Catherine Leendertz's maps are beautifully clear and they should help you to find your way around quite easily.

This book is for Bristolians and all who love the city as I do.

Helena Eason.

ACKNOWLEDGEMENTS

The following illustrations on pages 2, 27, 34, 44, 50, 53, 55, 71, 73, 78, 85 and 88, were taken by South West Picture Agency.

The photograph on page 62 is reproduced by permission of the City Museum and Art Gallery, Bristol.

Plate on page 22 supplied by Entertainments and Publicity Department, City of Bristol.

All other photographs by the Author.

CONTENTS

WALK 1

Bristol Bridge – High Street – Wine Street – Pithay – Tower Lane – Broad Street – Corn Street – Small Street – St. Nicholas Street.

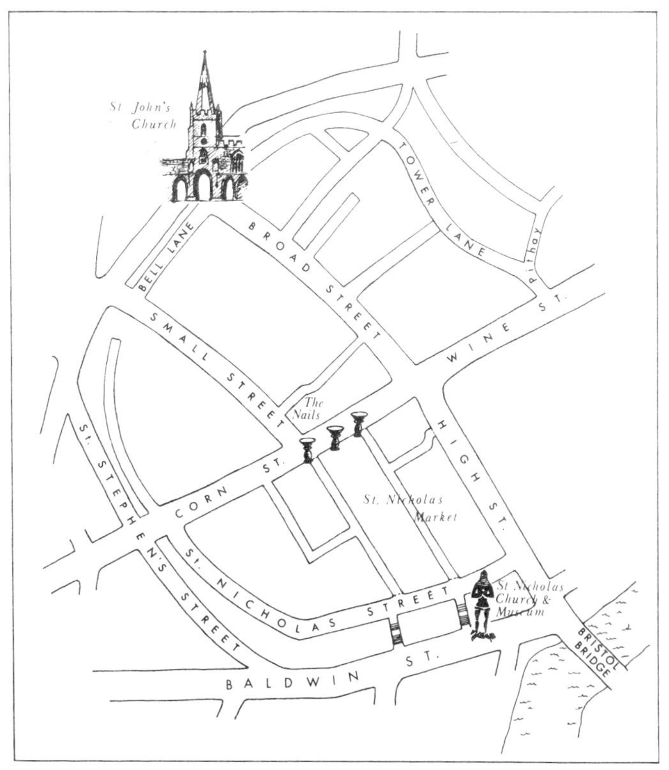

Your first walk in Bristol must begin with a look at the place where the city really started – **Bristol Bridge**.

From the very beginning of Bristol's history, the Avon has been crossed at this point and the very name, Bricgstow means, "place of the bridge". The first wooden bridge gave way in 1247, to a four-arched stone one. This was a fine bridge, like old London Bridge, with highly-desirable, highly-rated shops on either side, and in the centre a chapel of Our Lady of the Assumption. This bridge became increasingly too small for

Bristol Bridge

traffic but it was not replaced until 1768 when the present structure was built. The original graceful stone arches are partly concealed by the modern balustrading but the whole bridge is a busy thoroughfare into the old city. The city was originally entered through St. Nicholas Gate which has long since gone. The church of St. Nicholas which was over that gate is on your left and you will end your walk there.

As you walk up **High Street** you can admire the modern design of the Bank of England but the head of a staircase leading to a medieval cellar, now protected as an ancient monument, reminds us that this was one of the streets at the heart of the ancient city, so badly damaged during the 'blitz. You can see the tower of St. Mary-le-Port carefully restored, but the old timbered street itself is no more.

On the left, as you go up High Street, is the entrance to the Market. The classical frontage was built by Samuel Glascodine with John Wood the Elder, in a simple, dignified style. Although the entrance, with the City's Coat of Arms high upon the pediment is imposing, the market is best explored later from the St. Nicholas Street entrance. At the top of High Street, pause a moment and think back to the days when the old Civic High Cross stood here at the intersection of the four principal streets of the medieval town; High Street, Corn Street, Wine Street and Broad Street. This beautiful Cross, erected in 1373 when Bristol became a County, had niches in which were placed statues of the Kings who had given Bristol its Charters. It was at this spot that monarchs were proclaimed, and traitors were beheaded. The Cross was forty feet high and a timorous goldsmith in 1733 declared that his house and life were endangered by its swaying in the high wind. It was taken down, and in 1768 the Dean of Bristol impudently gave it to his friend, Henry Hoare, who used it as a focal point in the landscaping of his new house at Stourhead, where it stands today.

It is when you turn right at the top of High Street into **Wine Street** that you realise the extent of Bristol's architectural loss during the 'blitz for it was here that most of the merchants' timbered houses were built. The name itself is a corruption of Wynch Street, as the pillory once stood here. Wine Street has several historical associations. At Number 9, Robert Southey the poet was born in 1774, and a plaque on the wall of Christ Church recalls the spot where his father's linen-draper's shop once stood. His name is perpetuated in Southey House, an office block. As you walk along Wine Street you will see St. Peter's Church tower on the right but don't be tempted to cross over as you will be able to examine it and the castle area on your next walk.

On the left is a narrow lane called the **Pithay** which comes from the Norman word "puit" meaning a well and "hay" meaning a hedge or inclosure of stone, and the second wall that surrounded the old city was pierced here with a gate. All the ancient dwellings have been destroyed along with the thick Norman wall. The Pithay leads into **Tower Lane** on the left and though there are no remains of the towers left, the lane itself still curves along the old line. Go through the National Westminster Bank complex on the right and you will follow the narrow lane-line along the side of St. John's Church. This church is St. John the Baptist, also known as St. John-on-the-Wall as it was built over the original gateway, the last of the old city's seventeen gateways. The narrow nave runs alongside Tower Lane and was built into the old city wall, so there was no room for aisles. There has been a church here since 1174 but most of the structure is of the fourteenth century. If the church is open have a quick look at the recumbent effigy of Walter Frampton, the builder of the present church who died in 1388, and also at the unique pulpit hour-glass and eighteenth-century wrought-iron sword rest. The vaulted crypt is entered from Nelson Street and has been adapted for secular, parochial purposes. In Nelson Street also is St. John's Conduit which has conveyed water since medieval times from the top of what is now Park Street. There was a time after the 1940 'blitz when this conduit was the only water supply in the city. Do spend some time looking at this, the only remaining city gateway, through which Elizabeth I entered Bristol in 1574. On the **Broad Street** entrance are the figures of two Gaulish chiefs, Brennus and Belinus, who according to legend, founded Bristol in 390 B.C.

Now, walk up Broad Street, one of the original four main streets of the old city. Numbers 35 and 36 are well-preserved seventeenth-century houses and have an interesting fire-mark of 1711. Next to these houses is the entrance to the new National Westminster Court which is a good example of "good neighbourliness" in design, respecting the scale and character of surrounding buildings and retaining the pattern of medieval streets in an important corner of ancient Bristol. The Broad Street entrance has preserved the fascinating Everard Printing Works, the most complete decorated Art Nouveau building in Europe. Edward Everard wrote in 1900, "I am a printer heart and head and hand. Having in mind the century linking 1400 and 1500, when the daybreak of a new era was dawning out of the creation of Gutenberg, I elected to raise in Bristol a trophy contemporary with that period and with that genius. Coupled with this was the desire to repeat the salient features of St.

John's Gateway in this part of the city". He was an inspired conservationist long before that word became popular and this unique mosaic façade is the result. **John Street** is a narrow old street, with the Bank Tavern on one side and the last remains of St. James' Churchyard on the other. Number 41 Broad Street is

Down Broad Street

an eighteenth-century house with a notice visible on its cellar doors, "Shelter Exit" which reminds us that the old medieval cellars still exist in this area and were used during the war as Air Raid Shelters and now as storage cellars.

Another quiet little backwater is **Tailors' Court**, a reminder of the many seventeenth-century courtyards which existed in the city. Here, hidden away, is the Merchant Tailors Guild Hall built in 1745 and with the finest "shell" hood embodying their Coat of Arms. At the end of the court is another excellent Jacobean house, now known as Court House. Built in 1692 for I. F. Miller, a wholesale grocer, the shell hood incorporates his initials and date.

Opposite the court entrance is the Guildhall, now used for the Bristol Crown Court. This was built in 1846 in Tudor style on the site of the earlier medieval Guildhall where the notorious Judge Jeffreys held his infamous "Bloody Assizes" in 1685 after the Monmouth rebellion. This earlier Guildhall was also used for theatrical performances and legend has it that Shakespeare was a member of the Lord Chamberlain's Company which performed in the years 1587–1603. There is a record of the visit paid by his friend Edward Alleyne, so it is not impossible that Shakespeare himself also may have been here. The Crown Court sits on week-days 10–4 p.m. and though we no longer have the ceremonial attached to the old Assizes, the hearing of a Crown Court case is part of your educational experience and would interest anyone over sixteen. The Law Library incorporates portions of a thirteenth century house, the earliest example we have left of Norman domestic architecture.

At the top of Broad Street is Christ Church which is easily recognised by the eighteenth-century quarter-jacks of the clock which are loaned to the Church by the Corporation for 12½p per year! The hammers strike the quarter hour so you won't have long to wait to see the figures move. A church has been here since 1153 but the present one, a good example of later Renaissance architecture, was designed in 1786 by James Paty, and has a fine interior. The poet Southey was baptised here, as he was born round the corner in Wine Street.

Recently this area has been made into a pedestrian precinct and it makes your walk much more pleasant. You are now in **Corn Street**, the fourth in the original town plan. At the corner stands the old Council House, built in 1827 by Sir Robert Smirke, which was used for all meetings of the Bristol Council until the new one was opened on College Green. Before you go in, notice the statue of Justice, without her scales, with the City Arms on one side and the Royal Arms on the other, sculptured by E. B. Baily, the Bristolian whose statue of

Nelson tops the column in Trafalgar Square. Some of the rooms are now used as extra Crown Courts but if you wish to look around in some detail, have a word with the helpful porter at the main desk and he will let you know what to see. A good time would be a lunch hour and then you could gaze around the Court Rooms at your leisure. The main staircase leading up to the old Council Chamber is inlaid with brass and enamel, though it is often covered with a protective carpet. The old Council Chamber has oil portraits of visiting royalty including George I, Charles I, Queen Anne, William and Mary, and the famous Kneller portrait of James II. It was in 1851 when Jackson Curnock was cleaning these portraits that he saw an inferior head of Charles II painted on top of Kneller's portrait. He removed the paint and discovered the original James II which had obviously been painted over by an irate Protestant. On the walls of the New Council Chamber is an interesting collection of large paintings depicting famous events in Bristol's past history which are colourful, accurate and appealing. Underneath this Council House are the old cells of the Bridewell which once stood here, and though given a new coat of paint they are grim reminders of the justice meted out to prisoners in past centuries.

Next to the Council House is the 1858 Lloyd's Bank, a stunning building with its opulent Venetian design and sculptures. Its beauty goes some way to make up for the destruction of the Bush Inn, where Winkle came in his lovelorn quest of Arabella Allen in Pickwick Papers, which once stood here. Today, Corn Street is the centre of the banking world and it has always been a business centre. On the corner of Small Street and Corn Street was Lambert, the attorney's office where the poet Chatterton spent some miserable days.

Just stand back and admire the most beautiful Georgian building in Bristol; built in 1741 by John Wood, the Elder of Bath, a master of the Palladian style. It was intended to be the centre of activity for the commercial community, their Exchange. It was a great day for the city when it was opened and John Wood tells us that "the Keeper of Newgate carried the prisoners confined in that gaol for debt, to the Mayor's house, and Mr. Mayor, after releasing them at the Chamber's expense, gave each person something to begin the World with. He likewise ordered the Poor People in the Merchants Almshouse etc., to be entertained in a handsome manner, that the Hearts of all Denominations of men in the City might be cheer'd upon the day of opening this building". Despite its auspicious opening, incredibly the Exchange failed to attract merchants and they opened a new house opposite, in 1811, the Commercial Rooms. The Exchange itself was roofed over and became the Corn Exchange by which name it is still known. The Corporation grumbled at the expense of the glass roof because, "the farmers, a dilatory set of men would keep the Corn Merchants there much longer". You will be glad that they did cover in the colonnade especially on a Thursday afternoon when you can see the corn traders in action, buying and selling at their wooden desks. On a Friday morning, an Antiques and Craft Market is held here, but the building is open to the public at all times. Before you move off from this area, have another look at the whole building and notice the large clock. When this was started in 1822, Bristol time was ten minutes behind that of London. This meant that telegrams were received at the old Post Office on the right flank of the Exchange, apparently before they had been dispatched! The Railways also kept Greenwich time, so reluctantly the Corporation fixed a second minute hand to show Bristol and Railway time, but finally settled for "Cockney" time. On the left flank a Coffee House was built. Have you heard the expression, "to pay on the nail"? Well here in front of the Exchange are the original "nails" which gave rise to that expression. These nails were the historic brass tables used by merchants since the sixteenth century for their business transactions when they "paid on the nail". The oldest pillar is dated 1594 and they all have interesting inscriptions; the 1625 nail was given to commemorate its donor's deliverance from the Plague.

On the left of the Exchange is All Saints' Church, a good example of a small, city church set back in a quiet passageway. Again, this church is an old foundation, and there are four Norman pillars remaining in the nave, but most of the present building was begun after the disastrous 1466 fire which destroyed the oldest city reference library of the Kalenders. The most notable monument in the church is to Edward Colston, with a reclining figure carved by Rysbrack in 1721.

Take a quick look at the peaceful All Saints' Court with its seventeenth-century Glebe House or ancient parsonage, before you return to Corn Street and cross over into **Small Street**. This was, in former days, a street of important houses where illustrious visitors to the city were lodged, especially at Colston's house, a few relics of which are incorporated in the Law Library

Corn Street

of the Guildhall which occupies the site. Unfortunately all of these earlier houses have been demolished but the cellars of number 16 still exist and are in use in Foster's House where a plaque recalls the fact that this was the site of the house of John Foster, Mayor in 1481. The Assize Courts Hotel is new but it does contain an Elizabethan stone chimney piece from the old house which stood on this site, and where Charles I was once lodged. It was in this old house too that William Bonny set up the first provincial printing press in 1696 and indeed, the old Bristol Times and Mirror was printed here until 1868.

At the bottom of Small Street is another of the old lanes which originally ran inside the city walls, **Leonard Lane**. Near the top of the street is the entrance to Albion Chambers, where the legal profession has its home, reminiscent of the Temple chambers in London.

Back in Corn Street again, Bristol's "Lombard Street", you will see every bank represented including the latest, Coutts the Royal Bankers. Turn right at the bottom and visit St. Stephen's Church which is an archive of Bristol history. The city's part in Atlantic exploration is recalled by a wall monument, draped with mermaids and mermen to Martin Pring who sailed from Bristol in 1603 to New England under licence from Sir Walter Raleigh and there is a splendid recumbent effigy of Edmund Blanket and his wife. He was a fourteenth-century wool merchant but, contrary to popular belief, he was not the inventor of the blanket. The tall, western Tower, called by Ruskin, "one of the most stately gems of ecclesiastical art", was built in 1470 at the expense of John Shipward, four times Mayor. It really is a beautiful Gothic version of an old Italian campanile. The quiet churchyard area is typical of so many city churches, a place to rest and even eat your lunch on a fine day.

St. Nicholas Street follows the line of the old medieval street and it is this twisting curve which adds interest to many of the old streets in this quarter. On the left is the old Bristol Stock Exchange, now the Midlands and Western though still retaining the Bristol Coat of Arms above the entrance. This was a street of inns and the signs of some of them still colourfully remind us of the past. The Elephant, built 1863 keeps its superb trumpetting elephant sculpture and The Porcupine has a fine swinging sign. Before you turn up into the market look at the fountain erected in 1859 as the city's first memorial to Queen Victoria.

The St. Nicholas Market was built at the same time as the Exchange and consists of three arcades covered with a glass roof. The eastern arcade backs on to the Exchange and has an entrance into High Street which you noticed at the beginning of the walk. Originally only fruit and market produce was sold here, but now you can browse around stalls where china, books, leather goods and fabrics are sold cheaply. The Rummer, in the market has been a popular inn for centuries and there are records that a hostelry has stood on this site since 1241 when it was known as the Greene Lattis. It was in an inn on this site that Elizabeth I, Charles I, Charles II and Cromwell were known to have "rested". The present inn, the Rummer, was set back and rebuilt by John Wood when he erected the Exchange and designed the Market.

In St. Nicholas Street your walk ends at St. Nicholas Church. The church itself was badly damaged in the 'blitz but the vaulted medieval crypt was spared and the old city wall forms the south side of it. The real interest here is that this Church is now a Museum of Local History and Church Art where you could spend as much time as you like examining the many illustrations; old prints; old maps of Bristol; church plate and vestments. The most spectacular showpiece is the Hogarth Altar piece, the great triptych painted originally for St. Mary Redcliffe in 1755. Its three panels show the Sealing of the Tomb, the three Marys at the Sepulchre and the Ascension. There is even the actual receipt signed by William Hogarth to show that he was paid £525 for this now priceless masterpiece. On the upper level are relics from excavated sites and a series of maps and pictures which tell the story of Bristol's development.

In the Crypt is the Brass Rubbing Centre, a joy for children of all ages. Here there are exact replica brasses of all sizes from originals in local churches. Admission to the crypt is free, but a charge is made for the rubbing, which includes the cost of materials and varies according to the size. You could make a beautiful wall-hanging of a medieval knight in armour for a modest cost and half an hour's hard work. In the corner of the crypt is the tomb of John Whitson, the seventeenth-century philanthropist who founded the Red Maids' School for "forty poor women children to be under the care of some woman and taught to read English, to sew and to do other laudable work . . . and everyone of the said children to go apparelled in red cloth". Today the original forty has multiplied

St. Nicholas Fountain

ten times and the Red Maids' School is an important, Independent Girls' School.

As you finish your walk, look up at the clock face which is the only church clock in England with a second hand. From Norman times until 1939, the Curfew bell was rung nightly. In 1961 the bells were rehung and the curfew rings out once again at 9 p.m. Let us hope that you have finished your brass-rubbing before then!

WALK 2

Haymarket – Newgate – The Castle area – Penn Street – Broadmead.

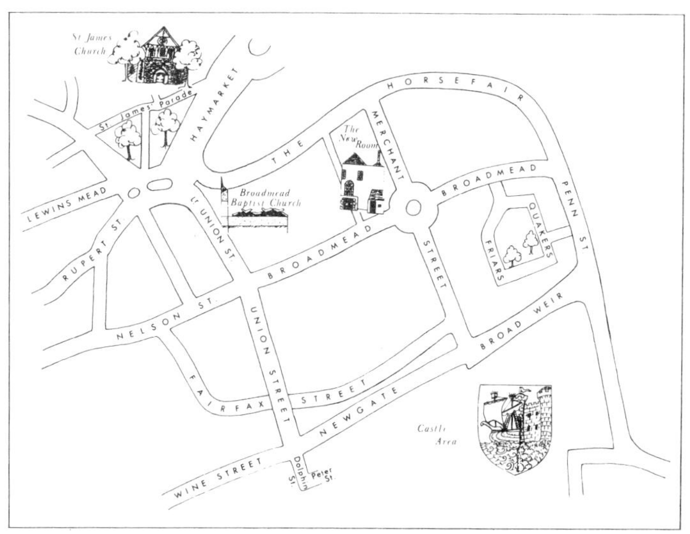

The Haymarket today is just another busy city highway, but until 1900 hay markets were actually held in St. James's churchyard itself; a road now covers the site, but the name remains to remind us of those bustling markets and horse-fairs.

St. James Church will be the starting point for this walk. The original Priory was erected in 1130 by Robert, Earl of Gloucester, and we are told that for every ten stones he imported from Normandy for the massive Castle Keep, he gave one stone for the building of this Priory Church. Originally, it had a cloister, dormitory and gatehouse, but it shared the fate of all monasteries at the dissolution in 1543 and its lands were bought up by developers. We are left with the fine Norman Church which has some unusual features. Look at the West Front entrance in Whitson Street, and at the Norman arcade of arches, three of which are pierced for circular headed windows, and at the small wheel window above, which is one of the earliest of its kind in England. The windows of the arcade are enriched with zig zag pattern moulding and the whole effect is solid and strong. The church is entered through the west front door. If the door is locked then obtain the key from the seventeenth-century Church House on the left. The interior of the church has been altered, perhaps not too successfully, but the twelfth century nave is sound enough. There are some exquisite, painted corbels supporting the roof timbers in the nave, showing the headgear worn in the twelfth century. They are rather high up, but don't miss them. A tomb discovered in the South Aisle is said to be an effigy of the founder Robert, Earl of Gloucester. The brief guide, at 5p, is worth buying if you want to know more about this, the oldest church in the present city.

On the corner of Whitson Street is the White Hart Inn, 1672, an old pilgrims' hostelry from the days when St. James' fair flourished in this area. The grass park in front of the church, St. James's Parade, is all that is left of the graveyard and fair ground but it has been made into a peaceful and pleasant garden in which to escape from the roar of the traffic. Don't be put off by the old story that this part of the Horsefair was a plague pit. When the area was built over in 1954, it is true that three hundred bodies were recovered and re-buried elsewhere, but they were found all four foot apart as in a normal burial, so that legend was destroyed.

Cross over at the pedestrian crossing and make for Lower Union Street. On your right is the new Broadmead Baptist Church, built in 1969 on a first floor site with shops beneath it. Though this church is modern there has been a Baptist church on this spot since 1671 and it is indelibly associated with non-conformist religious life in Bristol. It was here that Dorothy

Hazzard, disapproving of her clergyman husband's religion, started her own Baptist church in an upstairs room of her house and by the stairs in the new church is a symbolic rope handrail similar to that of her original church. A rope handrail had been fixed to help the elderly up the stairs, but when the civic authorities raided the illegal meeting, the congregation would sit on the stairs holding the rope thus obstructing the

White Hart Inn

magistrates and giving the preacher time to get away. The whole history of the Baptists in Bristol is contained in the Broadmead Records which tell of their early persecutions. This new building is better viewed from a distance when the thirteen ton finger pointing upwards, and the angels' wings flying above can be seen to greater advantage.

On your left is the Broadmead shopping precinct where you will end your walk. Continue up Union Street to its junction with **Newgate**. Here is the site of the old Newgate Gaol which John Howard the prison reformer, in 1775, called "white without and foul within". A plaque on the wall of the Co-operative Society building recalls, "Site of Newgate jail. Francis

Greenway, father of Australian Architecture, imprisoned here in 1812; Richard Savage, Poet and Playwright died here 1743" as a debtor.

This area was badly blitzed in 1940 but the Corporation has made an imaginative effort to reconstruct some part of the **Castle** area and with a little imagination and knowledge, we can visualise what this part of the city looked like in medieval times. It was here, just to the east of St. Peter's Church, that the old Saxon town of Bricgstow had its beginnings in ground later occupied by the Castle. Archaeologists digging in 1963 and 1975 have found evidence that Saxon houses were demolished to clear the site for the castle, which itself was demolished on Cromwell's orders in 1654.

St. Peter's church is now a ruin but it dominates the skyline at the edge of the castle area. The castle begun in 1126 was twice as big as Caernarvon Castle and covered this whole area. It had a great Norman Keep, larger than that of the Tower of London and within its walls a whole community of soldiers, smiths, armourers and suppliers lived guarding Bristol. If you look from St. Peter's towards the river you can see where the moat entered what is now the Floating Harbour. Near this entrance is the exit from an underground escape tunnel used by the castle defenders. Walk across to the castle mound and you can survey the whole area which this castle served. There are few visible remains but the precinct is at present being enclosed by a wall with bastions and vantage points which are evocative of the original site. There is one building which has been erected to preserve the small thirteenth-century vaulted vestibule of a much larger hall which survived the destruction and it may in the future house a small museum of relics from the castle site. Standing on this mound you can see why the castle was important, on a natural promontory with the valleys of the Frome and the Avon on three sides. The moat went round to the present **Broadweir** where until the eighteenth century the ducking stool stood and was used to dip scolds and shrews in the muddy waters.

Turn left at the corner of Broadweir and Penn Street and you will come into **Quakers' Friars**. How did this extraordinary name come about? The Friary was an old Dominican Friary which again was dissolved in 1542 and its lands sold. The

Quakers were a religious sect which suffered great persecution in the early days of their existence. One of these early Friends was Dennis Hollister a one-time Baptist who had "sucked in some upstart doctrines", and he gave a field "in the Friars" for a meeting place and here, in 1670, the Quakers erected their first house, in the ruins of the old Dominican Friary. It was here that William Penn, in 1696 married the granddaughter of

Quakers' Friars

Hollister, Hannah Callowhill, and a few years later they went to America and founded Pennsylvania, aided by Bristol Quakers' prayers and contributions. The present building was constructed in 1747 by George Tully and is rather an elaborate one for a meeting house, but the architect's friend Thomas Paty, had built the earlier New Room for the Wesleyans and set the plan for non-conformist meeting houses. Today, the Registry office has taken over the Quakers' Meeting Hall and the public can see the original hall in a well preserved state.

If you go round the left side of the office you will come to the Friary part of Quakers' Friars. First of all, call in to the Permanent Planning exhibition which the City Planning department has opened in the Bakers and Cutlers Halls. The plans, maps, pictures and models of old and new Bristol are fascinating in themselves but it is an added interest that they are housed in this old part of the Friary. Now, how did a Friary come to have a Bakers' and a Cutlers' Hall? Well, when the monasteries were destroyed and the Dominican friars expelled, their dormitory was taken over as a city Guildhall for the Bakers' Company in the sixteenth century, and the Friars' warming room became the Cutlers' Hall. The original thirteenth-century hammer-beam roof is there today and the whole building has been tastefully preserved, and more important, used. The actual marriage ceremony at the Registry Office takes place in the old Friary and the entrance is through the cloisters. In the vestibule is an interesting collection of relics from the old Friary including a fifteenth century stone coffin and lid.

Leave Quakers' Friars by the entrance into **Merchants Street**. This road was once known as Marshal Street, as it was the way taken by soldiers from the castle to their drill or marshalling grounds on Kingsdown. All the old houses were blitzed but one gem remains, the old Merchant Taylors' Almshouses, built in 1701 for nine poor tailors or their widows and daughters. Lloyd's Bank won a civic award for their careful preservation of the Almshouses which are a welcome addition to this modern shopping centre.

Turn left at the Hub into **Broadmead** and you are at the heart of the shopping precinct. This is a post-war development to replace the earlier shopping district in Castle Street and Wine Street. It has the merit of concentrating all the chain-stores and departmental shops in one area but architecturally it is a sad disappointment. There are, however, three places of interest which have been retained and over the years have settled down with their new neighbours.

The Greyhound Inn is an old coaching house and retains much of its links with the eighteenth century, including a nice "Bristol Union" firemark, though the old entrance for coaches has been destroyed. Opposite the Inn, set back in a courtyard, is a building with a stable at the side and an equestrian statue in the yard. This unpretentious looking house hides the New Room, a real place of pilgrimage open for all to see. John

Wesley's work in Bristol began at the request of George Whitefield who had met Wesley at Oxford, and shared his "methodist" views. Although Wesley was an Anglican, many churches had closed their doors against him and so Whitefield encouraged him to hold meetings in the open. These were so successful that they were anxious to find some permanent

St. James and Broadmead

meeting place, and on May 9th 1739 Wesley records in his journal, "we took possession of a field in the Broadmede".

So, here in Broadmead is the first Methodist Chapel in the world, opened as the New Room. The building has been restored to its original condition and the interior has panelled galleries, a spacious two-decker pulpit and a large clock for timing sermons. Incidentally, when Wesley was 85 he preached here without an assistant and writes that he was able, "to keep the meeting within the three hours". Above the hall are tiny living rooms used as bedrooms by Wesley and others, as he put it, "to bed and bait" themselves and their horses. Emphasis was very much on lay preaching and overlooking the pulpit was a window from which Wesley could, unseen, watch his preachers at work and help them. Outside is the stable where the horses could rest.

Americans pay homage to the New Room for it was here, at a conference in 1771, that Francis Asbury answered a call from the New World for a minister to come to them and the first Methodist chapel in New York was established. John's brother, Charles, the greatest hymn writer who ever lived, is closely associated with this place and his statue is in the north entrance in the Horsefair. Charles lived nearby in 4 Charles Street, behind St. James' Church where all his children were baptised and he himself buried.

The Arcade next to the Room is the one which survived the blitz, its partner was destroyed. It was built in 1824 as a covered shopping way for the new houses in the vicinity. It is really better than the famous Burlington arcade, as it is complete in every detail, as originally built. The entrance has fluted ionic columns and the shops have bow fronts. A ramp has replaced the steps but the whole arcade is colourfully restored.

Now, if you have any time left, enjoy some window-shopping or have a cup of tea in one of the many cafes in the precinct.

WALK 3

Bridgehead – King Street – Welsh Back – Queen Square – Prince Street – Narrow Quay.

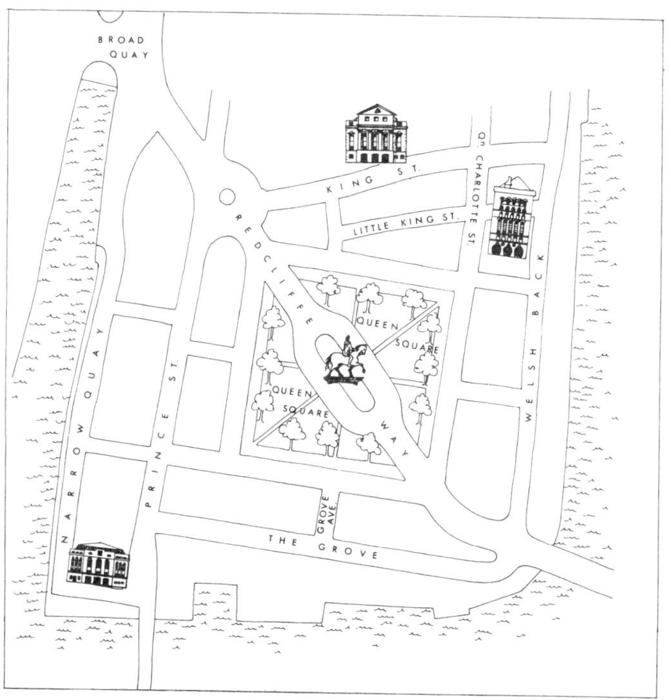

The Bridgehead is the starting point for this walk, so with a brief glance at the 17 storey Bristol and West Building, let us make straight for King Street and begin our adventure into the life of Bristol in the seventeenth and eighteenth centuries.

Here, in the "museum" street is a medley of architectural subjects of varying dates and styles spanning three hundred years. **King Street** itself marks the first move out of the old, walled, timbered city, by the prosperous merchants who

King Street Merchant Seamen's Almshouses

wanted to create a new residential area of spacious, elegant houses. It is a street which is visually exciting with a wealth of historic and literary associations. The Corporation has made a good effort at conservation here, preserving houses, cobblestones and street "furniture" wherever possible.

On the left as you enter the street is a pretty, pink-washed range of buildings on three sides of the original quadrangle. The Society of Merchant Venturers founded these residential Almshouses for sixteen old seamen in 1554 and it was enlarged in 1696 with money donated by Edward Colston. Read the poem painted on the board over the central dwelling, which will tell you why the Almshouses were built. As you go along King Street you will see the date 1699 on the side wall of the house and also the Coat of Arms of the Society of Merchant Venturers, including a mermaid with an anchor and Father Time with his scythe. Edgar Allan Poe founded his story, "The Gold Bug" on the life of one of these old sailors telling of strange territory in the Spanish Main and of hidden treasure.

King St. side view

The large building next door is the Old Library, opened in 1740 on the site of the original house offered by Robert Redwood to the city in 1614, for the purpose of establishing a free reference library. This was the second free public library in England, set up just five years after that of Norwich. The original house was soon outgrown and James Paty designed this Bristol Free Library which was used by many writers and poets, including Coleridge and Southey. This building was also outgrown in time and a new Municipal Central Library was erected in Deanery Road in 1906. On the old library wall is an old Parish boundary mark indicating the end of St. Nicholas parish and the beginning of St. Leonard's. There are still a few of these old marks left on buildings in the city and this is a particularly fine one.

One of the interests of King Street is the way in which houses of different centuries have settled down side by side. On the opposite side of the road is a group of seventeenth-century houses; Numbers 17, 18, 19 and 20 which has its original door still intact. On the left again is the nineteenth-century "Bunch of Grapes"; a Victorian warehouse, which is slightly florid in style but typical of many which have been lost; and then comes the Theatre Royal, the pride of Bristol. Opened in 1766, this is the oldest playhouse in Britain that has continued in use as such, and despite some minor changes this is the best surviving example of the larger town theatre of the eighteenth century. It was built to cater for the new sophistication of the merchant class and the Hotwells visitors and was deliberately erected outside the actual city, safe from the ruling of laws relating to "rogues and vagabonds". In 1778 George III granted a royal licence and gave the theatre the right to display the royal Coat of Arms.

If the Bristol Old Vic. Company is not rehearsing, do go in and have a look around. The interior was designed by James Paty in imitation of Sir Christopher Wren's Drury Lane theatre, but he did add a new touch, – the horse-shoe shaped auditorium. The colour scheme is the original green and gold and the whole effect is beautiful. Glance up at the roof space above the auditorium ceiling and visualise, though it is hidden, the original eighteenth-century "thunder-run", a sequence of wooden troughs down which cannon balls were rolled to give a most effective vibration of thunder. If you can, go up to the Gallery where there are several ranges of the original eighteenth-century backless, wooden benches, and imagine the vigorous gallery audience watching the first performance in May 1766, for which David Garrick wrote the prologue calling the theatre, "the most complete of its dimensions in Europe". Performances then began at half-past six and patrons were asked to send their servants by five o'clock to keep places!

The Theatre Royal was altered externally in 1972 and it

was a major achievement when the façade of the Coopers Hall, built by William Halfpenny in 1743, was restored as part of the new theatre complex. The Coopers, or Hoopers, was a trade organisation of barrel makers, an important craft in the city much concerned with such goods as wine, rum and sugar. Their hall dominates the street, with its façade of five bays and steep pediment displaying the Arms of the now defunct company. It is all the more valuable as it is the last of the eighteenth-century company halls remaining in Bristol and had been sadly neglected. Today it has been adapted internally as a foyer and recital room for the theatre with the chandelier and ceiling beautifully restored.

If you are a visitor to Bristol do try to see a performance by the Old Vic Company in this unique theatre. It could be the highlight of your visit.

The Tudor style building on the corner of King Street is St. Nicholas Almshouse, built 1652 and was the first building to be erected in the street. The trustees admirably restored it in 1961 and created ten flats here though they are not open to the casual viewer.

Now, cross the road and look towards Welsh Back. The eighteenth-century inn on the left is "The Old Duke", but it has a curiously modern sign. Do you recognise "the Duke" – Duke Ellington?

The old cobbled street leads to **Welsh Back**, where ships from Wales once berthed and merchants had their houses overlooking the river. These houses have disappeared over the years but the name remains to remind us of the sources of Bristol's trade and shipping. Walk across towards the River Avon and you will see why the Welsh Back was once a thriving thoroughfare. To the left you can see the heart of the old city with its bridge, ships, and church towers of St. Nicholas, St. Mary le Port and St. Peter. In front of you are the towers of St. Thomas and Temple churches with a glimpse of the new Shot Tower behind the Robinson building. To the right is "little Venice" with the warehouses reflected on the water and, in the distance, the spire of St. Mary Redcliffe. The capstans on the quay are the barrels of old cannon used in the Civil War 1645.

You passed a fine group of three houses on the right of King Street and the time has now come to take a more detailed look at them. These three are the remaining ones of a group of five built in 1664 as merchants' houses with underground cellars for goods unloaded at the Welsh Back. Today, the Llandoger Trow has the most notable half-timbered façade in the city. It takes its name from the trows (flat-bottomed barges) which came to the Welsh Back from Llandogo in the Wye Valley. This inn has been a haunt of sailors for centuries and tradition says that it was here that Daniel Defoe met the ship wrecked sailor Alexander Selkirk who had been brought back from the island of Juan Fernandez by Captain Woodes Rogers, and gave him the idea for "Robinson Crusoe". The Inn was indeed the haunt of such privateers as Woodes Rogers who lived round the corner in Queen Square. This superb Inn still has its original staircase, oak panelling and plaster ceilings.

Before leaving King Street, have a look at No. 6, a Queen Anne house with a magnificent shell-hood which with Nos. 7 and 8, restored seventeenth-century dwellings, makes a fine unit.

Go down Little King Street, and at its corner with Welsh Back, stand a while and admire the Old Granary. At one time the harbour was lined with tall warehouses of immense value to the urban scene but most of these were either blitzed or demolished; now the old Granary stands alone. Built in 1869 in polychrome brickwork it gave the name to "Bristol Byzantine" architecture, a style with a pointed arcade below, Venetian Gothic above, striped walling and Italian battlements as at the Palazzo Vecchio in Florence. It is now used as a Jazz Club, but the important building has been retained to grace the waterfront.

Continue along Queen Charlotte Street and into **Queen Square** itself. As you turn into Queen Square you enter a different world. This spacious square, enclosing an area of five acres, was begun in 1699 and named when Queen Anne visited the city in 1702. To make the square, the old Marsh was drained and the bear-baiting, archery and military exercises had to find another home while Bristol's domestic architecture itself was transformed. It was this Square, the first and finest example of planned building, which gave the lead to neighbouring Bath, just as later on Bristol was to copy the crescent from Bath.

If you walk around the Square, the largest in Europe, in a clockwise direction, you can note the varied architectural details which make this such an attractive place, for although two-thirds of the original houses were destroyed or damaged

Queen Square

during the 1831 Riots, enough remains to give an impression of the whole. No. 17 is perhaps a good house to stop and admire with its red brick restored to its original condition and the railings re-established. It was at No. 15 (now re-built) that David Hume, the philosopher, served his apprenticeship as a clerk to a prosperous merchant in 1734. This service ended when young Hume presumed to correct his master's correspondence and earned the rebuke, "I tell you what Mr.

Hume, I have made £20,000 by my English, and I won't have it mended!"

One of the first houses to be erected in the Square in 1699 for the vicar of St. Nicholas was No. 27, and this house and No. 28 have interesting shell-hoods to the doorways, while No. 29 has unusual key-stone masks. The Square was an important one in the eighteenth century and many countries had their consulates here; No. 37 has a plaque commemorating the first American consulate set up in Britain in 1792. Some of the next houses have sadly degenerated into warehouses but No. 51 is coming up to interest you. Take a closer look at its portico and Phoenix sculpture on the parapet, and remember that this was the house in which Ellen Terry lodged when she was playing at the Theatre Royal. Did she use that quaint, old, iron Dolphin footscraper?

In 1935 the Square was bisected by the arterial road. In the middle of the road is the famous equestrian statue of William III by Michael Rysbrack. In 1736 the Bristol Whigs decided to erect, "a public statue to the memory of a great and glorious Deliverer, William III". It is Rysbrack's masterpiece and during the war years, Queen Mary had it removed to Badminton for safe keeping.

After you have had a closer look at this statue in its dominating position, note the large building in front of you. This is the Custom House, built in 1836 to Sydney Smirke's design after the original one had been utterly destroyed by the 1831 Rioters, its fine façade and Coat of Arms add dignity to this side of the Square. Now, turn back and cut down Middle Avenue to Prince Street, sadly decayed from what it was in the days when select houses here were much in demand by Bristol's prosperous businessmen. There is still one group of three houses, Nos. 66, 68, 70, built 1725, which remains to give a picture of the one-time grandeur of this street. The Unicorn Hotel was the first of the city's post-war motels and though attractive in its own right, it hardly makes up for what has been lost.

Turn left into **The Grove** noticing the prison-like seed warehouse on the corner, and make your way past other warehouses to the end of the Grove where you will get your best view of the Inn on the corner. This Inn, the Hole in the Wall, has a commanding view of the waterside and was known in press-gang days, as the Coach and Horses. There were many dangers for seamen in Georgian Bristol but the most notorious was the Press-gang on the prowl for sailors to man the ships. Take a closer look at the little building jutting out a yard or two, with the narrow slits at eye-level and you will see how fortunately this building was sited. When the press-gang was seen, the look-out in this building gave the alarm and the sailors left the inn quickly by the back entrance and were lost in the Square.

You are constantly reminded of the importance of the sea in Bristol's history on this Walk, with this Inn, its neighbour the Bristol Sailors' Home and the ships in the Floating Harbour.

Back in Prince Street again and you are surrounded by water. Children especially will love the variety of shipping, dockside equipment and general activity of this area and a good "haven" for children and adults alike would be the Arnolfini Gallery. This building was originally the Bush tea warehouse, dating from 1840 and typical of the best Industrial Architecture of the area. Tough, strong, plain with robust Florentine detail it now houses the Arnolfini contemporary Arts complex. This adaptation of an old warehouse has re-vitalised this area and is well worth a visit. You can admire the contemporary paintings, jewellery, sculpture on permanent display; browse round a good bookstall and print shop; check on films in the cinema and other performances, and then have a welcome snack or drink in the bars and restaurant. The whole complex is open to everyone Tuesday to Saturday from 11 a.m.

As you come out into Narrow Quay, you are now at the end of your walk and you can take your time in this quiet backwater of the city docks. At all times of the day there are ships of all shapes and sizes moored here, and often visiting ships are open to the public. Narrow Quay leads into Broad Quay where you started.

WALK 4

Bristol Bridge – Victoria Street – St. Thomas Street – Temple – Redcliff Street – Guinea Street – Bathurst Basin – "The Great Britain".

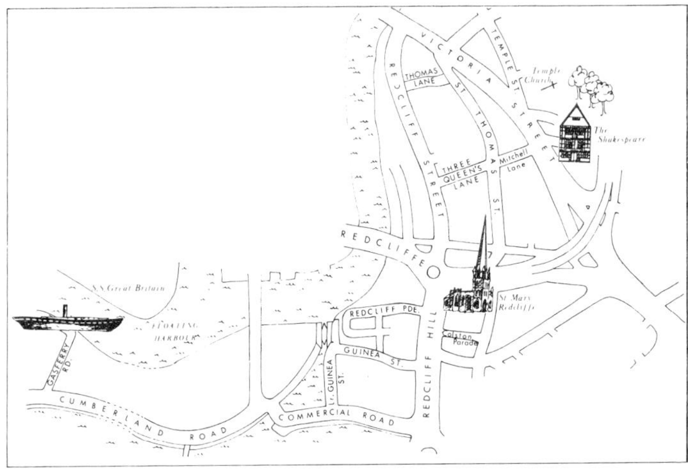

At one time, Redcliff and Temple parishes were suburbs separated from Bristol by the Avon, but in 1240, Henry III "saluted his honest men of Redcliff and commanded them to help his beloved men of Bristol to lend a hand in making the Quay". This royal command was obeyed and the river Frome was diverted through Canons' Marsh to join the Avon near the present Bathurst Basin in order to provide a harbour near the town centre. This was a colossal engineering feat in the thirteenth century and for their efforts, Redcliff and Temple parishes were incorporated into the town thus doubling the area of Bristol.

If you start at Bristol Bridge you can look back at the original town before crossing over into this area. **Victoria Street** was cut in the nineteenth century and on the left is one of the few rows of Bristol "Byzantine" shops and warehouses left in the city. At this time they are derelict and unless the Department of the Environment has a change of heart, they will disappear to be replaced by office blocks. However, nestling in the shade of the Robinson Building, the first fifteen storey office block to be built in 1964, is a pleasant group of four seventeenth-century houses, relics of the domestic architecture of this once prosperous suburb. Next to these houses is **St. Thomas Street** once the most important thoroughfare out of the town. Now little remains of its former glory except the church of St. Thomas the Martyr, originally built in the thirteenth century but re-designed in the eighteenth. The altar-piece of 1716 survives as an example of the ones that adorned many of the parish churches in the prosperous days of the eighteenth century. The most famous one is the altarpiece painted for St. Mary Redcliffe by William Hogarth and now in the St. Nicholas Church Museum.

To the right of the church is the narrow **St. Thomas Lane** and the Seven Stars Inn. It was here in 1787 that Thomas Clarkson sat and learnt a good deal from the landlord, who showed him some of the haunts frequented by seafaring men when the slave trade was flourishing. He gathered information in this Inn from local sailors about the iniquitous slave traders, which he passed on to his friend William Wilberforce who used it to further his cause, the Abolition of Slavery.

Return to Victoria Street again and you come to **Temple** Church. The Knights Templars were given some marshy land in 1145 here, on which they built their original oval-shaped church. When the Order was suppressed in 1312, the Church was taken over by the Knights of St. John who destroyed the oval church and built the present one. Only the shell of the church survived the 'blitz but the whole structure is maintained by the Ministry of Public Buildings and Works and is in good condition. The key can be obtained from the Bristol Boat Centre, opposite, and it is quite an interesting experience to walk around this ruin and remember that this was the church of the prosperous fourteenth-century weavers containing their ancient Guild Chapel, and serving an area noted for its weavers, fullers, dyers and tuckers employed in the cloth trade which once flourished here. The most unusual part of the church is the tower, 113 feet high but 5 feet out of true. Begun in 1300, the tower subsided when it was half completed and work was suspended for sixty years. This gave rise to the fiction that the

Shakespeare Inn and Temple Church

tower subsided because it was built on woolsacks. This was a misreading of the fact that it was metaphorically, not literally, built on woolsacks, the money from the wealthy wool trade providing the funds for building the tower. You can see how out of true this leaning tower is by comparing it with the new office block on the left. The medieval part of Temple Street was destroyed by the late nineteenth-century building of Victoria Street, but recent excavations on the now derelict areas around the church have unearthed the remains of houses dating from the fourteenth century and the sites of the timber racks used for drying cloth. The hooks used for attaching the cloth to the racks were known as tenter-hooks, and this gave rise to the expression, "to be on tenter-hooks". The area is due to be built over but at least the excavations and its discoveries have been recorded and are on display in the City Museum. The gardens around the church are sufficiently secluded for you to forget that the main road to Bath is a few yards away.

Temple Street once possessed more licensed premises than any other street in Bristol and there is one hostelry remaining from the seventeenth century. The Shakespeare 1636, makes a focal point for the few surviving seventeenth century houses on this once busy coaching route out of Bristol. The façade is original and well preserved though its neighbours are decayed. If you cross over Victoria Street and cut through Mitchell Lane and Three Queens' Lane you come into Redcliff Street. This street also has lost its former glory but at the top you will get a view of St. Mary Redcliffe which should make up for this dismal approach.

St. Mary Redcliffe, though it looks like a Cathedral is a parish church, "the fairest, goodliest and most famous parish church in England" said Queen Elizabeth when she visited Bristol in 1574. It is indeed accepted as the finest example of Gothic architecture in England, "the pryde of Bristowe and the Western londe". Its position on the red cliffs above the docks at the very centre of shipping and industry, is the key to its history. Since 1180, merchants had begun and ended their journeys and voyages at the shrine of Our Lady of Red Cliff, and to them and especially to William Canynges, five times Mayor of Bristol, we owe the church as it is now. Its beautiful spire however was struck by lightning in 1445 and it was not replaced until 1872 when a Mayor and Mayoress with a good head for heights climbed up 293 feet to fit the capstone on the new one. The church is best entered by the North Porch; the inner porch is the oldest part of the fabric and the outer is one of the loveliest examples of the decorated style, hexagonal in shape. At one time it housed a relic of the Blessed Virgin Mary, past which pilgrims filed through the smaller doors. Above, is the Muniment Room where the youthful Chatterton found parchments and church manuscripts on which he wrote his Rowley poems. Opposite the church in Redcliffe Way is Chatterton's birthplace with the front of Pile Street school where his father taught, attached to it. You can view the outside but the interior can only be seen by prior arrangement with the City Museum.

St. Mary Redcliffe

There are so many fascinating things to see in St. Mary Redcliffe that it is difficult to know what to single out. You must not miss the painted wooden statue of Elizabeth I; the rib of a whale thought to have been brought back by Cabot after discovering Newfoundland; the memorial tablet to Admiral Sir William Penn, father of the founder of Pennsylvania, together with his armour and battle flags; and the two tombs of Canynges, one in rich merchant's robes and the other in priest's robes. If you have time, buy the excellent guide book and with its aid explore this superb church in detail. Leave by the South Porch and wander round the churchyard and see the tombstone commemorating the family of Thomas Chatterton; the nearby grave of the celebrated church cat who served for fifteen years as the church mouser; and the half-impaled tramline which was blown over the houses from Redcliff Hill by a wartime bomb.

In **Colston's Parade** is Fry's House of Mercy, an almshouse established in 1784 for eight poor women, yet another almshouse in a city noted for its charitable foundations. A tablet on No. 9 put up by the Merchant Venturers, states that, "Here was born on 10th day of February, 1824, Samuel Plimsoll, the originator of the Plimsoll Line". Plimsoll never forgot the sight of the over-loaded vessels in the docks and when he became an M.P. he worked to get his Merchant Shipping Act passed in 1876 enforcing a "load-line" on every ship. His slogan was, "man's greatest safeguard is publicity".

At the top of **Redcliff Hill,** set low down in the church wall, is the Conduit, given in 1190 as a water supply to the church, by Lord Robert de Berkeley, whose effigy in chain mail is in the north transept of the church. Every September, the clergy walk the whole length of the pipe, to its source in Knowle, in a lively ceremony to assert the church's right to this water. You will have to cross over this busy road at the roundabout and on the other side, set into an outcrop of the red cliff, is the garden that in 1665 was granted to the Society of Friends by Charles II, as a Burial Ground and used as such until 1921. Today it is a pleasant garden for the Blind, planted with sweet smelling herbs. At the back of the garden is a low, pointed arch in the rock which leads into a small cave with the imposing name of St. John's Hermitage. From 1346 to 1669 it was indeed occupied by a succession of hermits living a life of seclusion among pleasant fields which once sloped down to the Avon. The whole of this red cliff is riddled with caves, most likely the result of quarrying the sandstone for the local glass and pottery industries in the eighteenth century. This network of caverns extends almost to the church but they are closed except to conducted parties as the lone explorer would soon get lost.

As you walk up Redcliff Hill, look at the head offices of the

Phoenix Assurance Company with the nicely enclosed open space fronting on to Guinea Street. In the Reception area of these offices is the 200 year old fire engine originally built for St. Mary Redcliffe at a cost of £35. **Redcliff Parade** is in the process of restoration and it is worth while pausing here for a moment to look over the city and pick out the now familiar landmarks of, from left to right, the Cathedral, the Cabot Tower, the University, Christ Church, St. Nicholas, the Robinson Building, the Shot Tower, Temple Church and St. Mary Redcliffe. Did you spot them all?

Bathurst Basin

At the corner of Albert Place and **Guinea Street** is an old eighteenth-century house, with a wooden chair fixed above the door. This was once an inn with the unique name, The Old Armchair. The most important remaining houses in Guinea Street are Nos. 10, 11 and 12, orignally built as one house for a thriving merchant, Captain Edmund Saunders, in 1718. The key-blocks have the most varied carvings in Bristol; eagles, dolphins, parrots, even an Irish harp. The next large building is the Bristol General Hospital built in 1853 to take care of casualties from the docks and the new factories, at a time when Guinea Street was a healthy spot surrounded by water away from smoke-filled streets. The hospital, built in "warehouse" style of the Italian Renaissance won an architectural competition for its designers Gingell and Lysaght. They had the bright idea of constructing the basement to provide 8,000 square feet of warehouse space which could be let to merchants using the Bathurst Basin and thus providing an income for the hospital.

On the corner is the old Ostrich Inn, built in 1775 with benches outside where old salts quenched their thirst. If it's a warm day you can do the same and enjoy the view of the Bathurst Basin, an inland waterway typical of Bristol. Amateur sailors berth their boats here and there is always some activity to watch. There are some good old warehouses, cranes unloading sand and gravel, and the old lock gates and swing bridge to admire. In the seventeenth century this water was known as Treen Mills and once a year the Mayor and Corporation would hold their annual Duck shoot here. You will find plenty of seagulls today, but they're a bit short on ducks.

Lower Guinea Street leads into Commercial Road and **Cumberland Road.** On the right is the Bathurst Tavern built in 1800 when the view over the surrounding countryside was extensive. This view inspired the designer to include first floor balconies with iron standards and railings reminiscent of New Orleans. Though the view has disappeared, the Tavern stands proud at the entrance to the Basin. The old ruin on the right is the Gatehouse of the Old Gaol built in 1820 to replace the dreadful Newgate. It was this gaol that was the target of the 1831 Rioters who burnt down the Governor's quarters, released the prisoners and destroyed the treadmill. This Gateway was the scene of the last public hanging of a woman in Bristol, when in 1849 Sarah Thomas was hanged for murder.

As you walk along Cumberland Road you will see direction signs, "To the Great Britain", and further along the road at **Gas Ferry Wharf** this famous ship is berthed. It was this dock that Brunel originally constructed for the building of his first iron ship with a screw propeller, and from this dock Prince Albert launched it in 1843. The hulk was salvaged in 1970 and brought back from the Falkland Islands to its original home where it is undergoing restoration to show what life was like on board an ocean-going Victorian liner. The ship, dock and

Old Gaol Gatehouse, Cumberland Road

museum are open all the year as is the restaurant and souvenir shop.

Alongside the car-park is the "Bristol Packet", a lovely canal boat which from Easter to September takes visitors on a trip round the docks. This would be a delightful way to see some of the outstanding buildings in Bristol. After your trip, take another form of transport back to the Centre, the new horse-drawn bus or walk back along Commercial Road into Prince Street and the Centre.

WALK 5

St. Augustine's Parade – Colston Avenue – Christmas Steps – Haymarket – St. Michael's Hill – Royal Fort – Park Row.

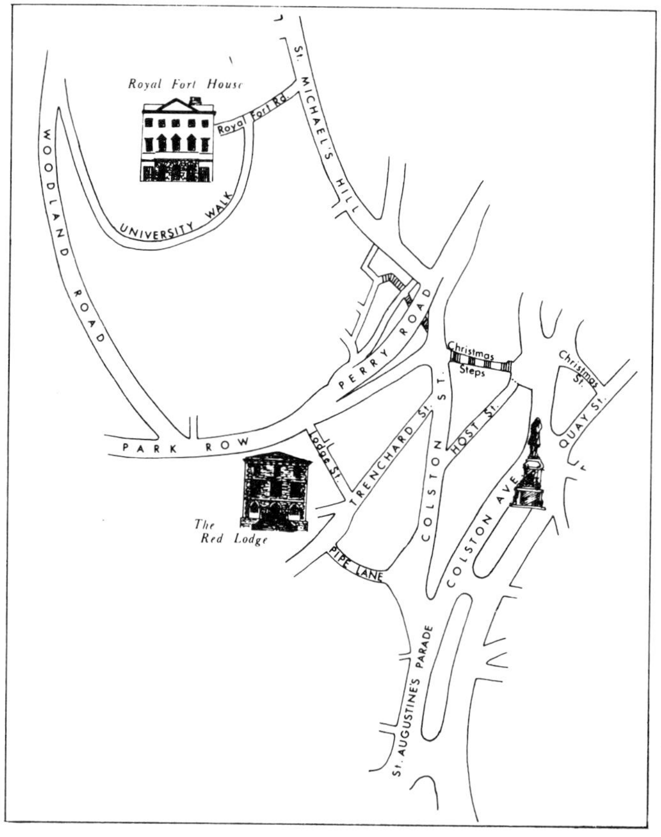

Although it is officially called **St. Augustine's Parade**, for most Bristolians it will always be the Tramways' Centre as it was here in 1875 that the first tramline was laid and Bristol's traffic problems began. The trams have disappeared but the name remains and so do the cars which took over. The Centre area itself was actually built in three stages by covering over the River Frome which at one time flowed right through the city. The river runs underground today, but until 1892 ships could sail right into the centre of the city. The gardens look splendid with the flowers in full bloom, but one must regret the loss of ships in full sail.

There are some old eighteenth-century houses in St. Augustine's Parade which have stood up well to their adaptation as shops. The Drawbridge Inn reminds us that a drawbridge was until 1827 necessary in order to cross the river at this point. The Hippodrome opened in 1912 for the presentation of spectacular musicals, opera and variety shows, but like so many of the larger theatres it is threatened with closure. The offices of the Tramways Company are perhaps over-restored timber frame seventeenth- and eighteenth-century houses, but they form a colourful group at the end of the Parade.

Cross over the pedestrian crossing and ahead of you is Magpie Park, so called because a scurrilous weekly newspaper, the Bristol Magpie, was once published near here. The city is well blessed with statuary and here Edmund Burke, the M.P. for Bristol 1774–1780 raises his arm in greeting to the citizens reminding them that "taxation without representation" would lose Britain her American colonies. Burke however, rarely visited Bristol claiming that, "you choose a Member indeed; but when you have chosen him, he is not a Member for Bristol, he is a Member of Parliament".

Edward Colston was Bristol's most liberal philanthropist and his name is remembered everywhere in the city. His statue is interesting with dolphins rising at the corner of each plinth. The plaques show a group of sailors finding a dolphin which had plugged a hole in their leaking ship, enabling them to reach their home port safely with the valuable merchandise which allowed their owner to carry out his charitable works. Not far away is the 1932 Cenotaph, plain and dignified, where pigeons are fed by kindly old ladies and senior citizens take their rest.

On the left is a lovely church, the Roman Catholic St. Mary's on the Quay, its name reminding us that it was once actually on the quay when the river Frome flowed along here. The church was originally built for the Irvingites, an evangelical sect, in 1839 and bought by the Catholic community a few years later. The classical exterior and Corinthian portico dominate this side while the interior is most attractively finished in green and gold. On the wall is a memorial to the parishioners who died in the 1914–18 War, and the first name is that of G. Archer-Shee, the original of the naval cadet in Terence Rattigan's, "Winslow Boy". As you leave St. Mary's just glance along Quay Street and you will see the remains of the last old city wall with St. John's Church and gateway.

Your route lies to the left of Electricity House making for the Christmas Steps area, perhaps the most picturesque part of old Bristol. **Host Street**, originally Horse Street, was for centuries the only direct way from the city, via St. John's Gate, to St. Augustine's, and its junction with Christmas Street was a fine place to witness spectacular civic and royal pageants. Over the years, Host Street has deteriorated but the whole area is now a conservation area and its future seems assured. Here, at the bottom of **Christmas Steps**, is the original entrance to the fourteenth-century convent for old sailors, known as St. Bartholomew's Hospital. The archway itself is architecturally unique, being struck from four centres and therefore depressed in form. On one side of the exterior is a mutilated figure of the Virgin and Child. After the dissolution of the Monasteries, the Hospital estates were purchased by the executors of Robert Thorne and given in 1532, to the Mayor and Corporation for the provision of a free Grammar School, "with a master and ushers to teach grammar to all children and others that would repair for learning and knowledge of the Latin tongue and other good learning, and for the better education and bringing up of youth in knowledge and virtue". Above the doorway is a seventeenth-century house where the school remained until 1769 when, in a scandalous exchange by the Corporation, the Grammar School was moved to more spacious premises in Unity Street belonging to Queen Elizabeth's Hospital and that school was left in wretched surroundings here until 1847. It was outside this archway that the Grammar School boys greeted Queen Elizabeth in 1574 as she made her way up Host Street to the Cathedral. Three boys were to read long speeches depicting Salutation, Gratulation and Goodwill, but after hearing the first two the Queen's own goodwill seemed to evaporate and

Chapel of the Three Kings of Cologne

she decided to move on to Sir John Young's Great House, where the Colston Hall now stands, and to a week of more congenial entertainment.

Christmas Street was originally a rugged, stony path that followed the boundary wall of St. Bartholomew's estate, and has been variously known as Cutlers' Street, Knifesmith Street,

Queen Street, and by 1774, Christmas Steps. The steps themselves were erected in 1669 by a public-spirited Sheriff, Jonathan Blackwell when he set the street out in two slopes and three sets of steps, at his own expense. At the top of the steps you can sit in one of the niches and read the memorial to him, and be thankful that this street was, "steppered, done and finished" in 1669. The road itself has a variety of houses of different styles and date but the whole effect is harmonious, and you will want to spend some time looking at the antique shops, coin shops and even a joke emporium. You will be glad of that little rest at the top!

John Foster was a wealthy salt-merchant, who, in 1484, erected an almshouse for, "one priest, eight poor men and five poor women". The original almshouse has been rebuilt three times on the same site and the one at the top of the steps is the 1863 version in the Burgundian style with ornamental turrets, open spiral staircases with candle-snuffer roofs and projecting corner oriels. The diaper-patterned brickwork with stone dressings makes the whole group an artistic triumph. The accompanying Chapel of the Three Kings of Cologne is a unique dedication, built in 1504, for the inmates of the almshouse. It is only 18ft. by 22ft. and is open to the public.

Cross over at Colston Street traffic lights into Upper Maudlin Street. The huge Bristol Royal Infirmary complex is on your right, but turn up by the King David Hotel into **St. Michael's Hill**.

This road was one of the first to be built out of the city in the late seventeenth century when merchants wished to live away from the crowded heart and it is full of interest architecturally. The road takes its name from the church of St. Michael the Archangel but this church has been so altered that it has little appeal left except the original perpendicular tower, although the trees, lanes and open spaces around it create a peaceful oasis high over the city. On the left, off a wide pavement raised many feet above road level, are Georgian houses, restored by the University and used by it. The whole hill is now virtually part of the University precinct and much successful restoration has been done in recent years. Perhaps this is not altogether out of keeping with the educational spirit of the place, for the eighteenth century saw many of the fine houses used as schools trading on the healthy air of the hill, where many notables, including Charles Kingsley and Robert Southey received their education.

On the right are some fine old inns; the Colston Arms; the Scotchman and his Pack, but the loveliest building in a lovely street is the Colston Almshouse set round three sides of a

St. Michael's Hill Pavement

quadrangle with stuccoed walls and red pantiled roofs with pediments over doors and windows, and a charming bell-cote. Edmund Colston was a West Indies merchant who, though born in Bristol, lived most of his life at Mortlake in Surrey but never forgot his birthplace, giving over £80,000 to various charities and a school. In 1695 he erected this almshouse for twelve men and sixteen women, stating that he, "would willingly that they should be such as have lived in some sort of decency; but that a more especial regard should be had that none be admitted that are drunkards; nor of a vicious life or turbulent spirit, lest the quiet order that the inhabitants at present live in be thereby interrupted".

All the houses on the hill are different and you will find your own favourite. No. 46, dated 1711 is a fine stone house in a splendid state of preservation.

On the left is the name, Tankard's Close, originally Stinkard's Close, where in the seventeenth-century plague houses were built where all persons coming from a plague area were obliged "to air themselves" for thirty days in a vain attempt to keep the disease out of the city. At the top of the

Colston's Almshouses

Close is Rupert Gate, the gate by which Prince Rupert left the Fort in 1643, when he swept down to the city. Before you actually go through the gate, look back over Bristol and you will see why this area was such a desirable one in the eighteenth century. It was also the route to the public gallows further up the hill, and there were many and bitter complaints from the residents about the "loud, noisy and vicious behaviour" of the spectators on their way to the entertainment.

As part of the City's defences during the Civil War, a number of forts were built on the hills surrounding the centre and the largest of these was the Windmill Fort. After Prince

Rupert had captured the hill from the **Parliamentary** forces in 1643 its name was changed to the Royal Fort and 22 guns, a powder magazine and a barracks were added. After the Civil War was over, the land and park was bought up by Thomas Tyndall and in 1767 the Royal Fort House was built for him by Thomas Paty. The link-extinguishers and iron work flambeau holders are most attractive but the real treasures of the house lie in the interior and the elaborate stucco-decorations by Thomas Stocking in the staircase hall. Here you can see the finest examples of the characteristic features of the Bristol school of eighteenth-century plasterers; a bird, usually a stork, modelled in high relief and standing away from the main design. The University Music Department uses this house, but interested members of the public could look around the house and the gardens, which were originally laid out by Humphrey Repton as part of the larger Tyndall's Park. Opposite the Fort House is the Physics Building which from a distance presents a turret-like appearance and resembles a fort itself.

You come out of the Royal Fort into University Walk with the new buildings of the Grammar School to your right. You saw the original school in Christmas Steps and here, four hundred years later, is the fine Independent school with a tradition of scholarship.

Turn left into Woodland Road and down into **Park Row**, leaving the University area itself for another walk. At the junction of Park Row and Lodge Street, almost overshadowed by a multi-storey car park, is the entrance to the Red Lodge. This Lodge was one of the two original lodges which stood in the gounds of the Great House which Sir John Young built in 1590 on the site of a Carmelite Priory which he had purchased after the dissolution of the monasteries. The Great House, in which Queen Elizabeth I had stayed, was itself destroyed in the nineteenth century and the Colston Hall built on the site, but the Red Lodge was saved and is now a Museum, open every afternoon from 1 to 5 p.m. The finest Elizabethan panelling in England is to be seen here, a survivor of the kind of domestic opulence that the first generation of Merchant Venturers delighted in exhibiting. The inner porch to the large room was richly carved by an Italian craftsman and the whole house is furnished in Elizabethan and Jacobean style. Another interesting use for the house came in 1854 when Lady Byron, the poet's widow, bought the Lodge for Mary Carpenter who set up a school here for girls from the streets. This school, or "reformatory" was the first of its kind in the country and flourished until 1919.

Now, if you go down Lodge Street, built in 1763, you can see what happens to streets which have been neglected and vandalised. This terrace was once a fine example of the work of Thomas Paty, but today it is a silent witness to the urban desolation which can come from neglect and lack of vision. You are now behind the Colston Hall and you can either go along **Pipe Lane** and into the Tramways Centre, or, if you have the strength, turn right to the Mecca Entertainment Centre and ice-skate, see a film, dance, or play Bingo – according to the state of your feet and/or purse!

WALK 6

Counterslip – Old Market Street – Portland Square – Brunswick Square – Somerset Street – Kingsdown Parade.

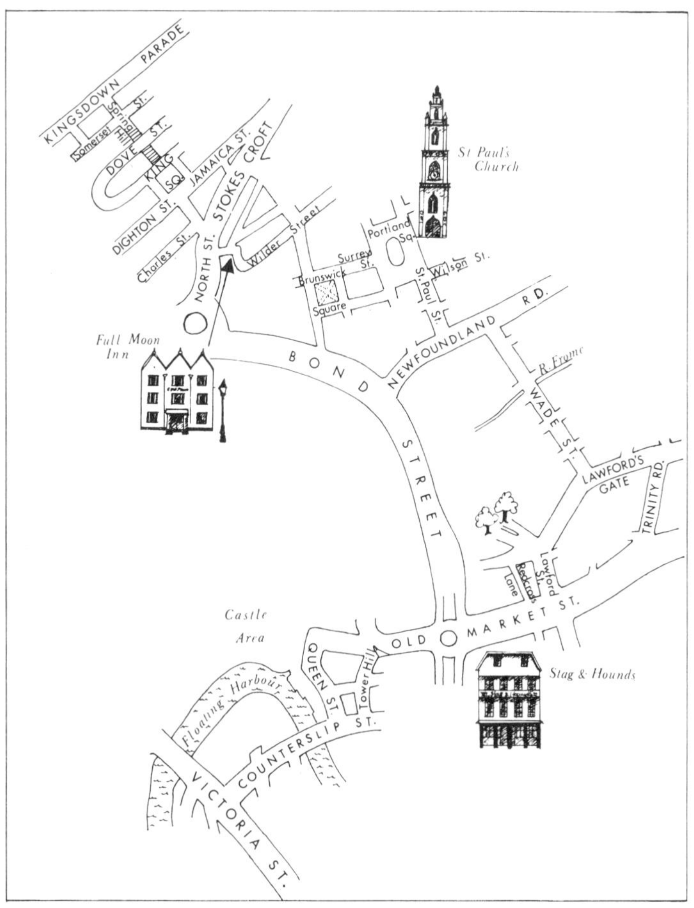

On this walk you will see the development of Bristol outside the original city walls in the eighteenth and nineteenth centuries. It is, however, a sad tale you will hear of demolition, desolation and destruction. There is enough left to interest you, and indeed to make the walk worthwhile, but you will finish by echoing Othello's words on his own tragedy, "oh, the pity of it all, the pity of it all".

As you leave Bristol Bridge and face Victoria Street, the first road on your left is Counterslip, a corruption of Countess's Slip, as this area was once a riverside ferry-crossing belonging to the Countess of Salop. Today, Courages' slip would be a better name as that famous brewery has taken over the site. There are many new buildings in Counterslip, including the very modern Fire Station and the Sheldon and Bush Patent Shot Company, with its 141 foot tower, a notable landmark in Cheese Lane. The original shot-tower was built in 1782 on Redcliff Hill by William Watts, a plumber who made his fortune from a discovery which came to him in a dream. He saw perfect, spherical shot being made by allowing droplets of molten lead to fall from a great height into water. He used his wife's vegetable collander to carry out tests which proved so successful that he constructed a tall tower over his house to produce lead shot on the same principle. His original house and tower was demolished in 1970 and this one built where molten lead is still poured through small holes, down a 120 foot drop into water in the same way.

You can get yet another good view of the Castle area from St. Philip's Bridge on your left. The moat exit, into the river, the old warehouses down to the water's edge, and St. Peter's Church still standing defiantly add a touch of life to this rebuilt district. If you turn up **Queen Street** you come directly onto the Castle Mound and get a sight of the old city with the spires of St. Peter's, St. Mary le Port, St. Nicholas, All Saints and Christ Church jostling one another on the horizon. Today you have a clear view but until 1940 Castle Street was full of stores and late-night bargain hunters in this most popular shopping centre. The destruction of the 'blitz was a terrible blow, but the imaginative reconstruction of the Castle park as an open space is certainly a bonus in this rather drab area.

As you turn right into **Tower Hill**, you can see the church of St. Philip and St. Jacob (once St. James), marooned on a traffic island. This is not altogether incongruous, as when it was built in 1193 it was a country church with a spacious, peaceful graveyard away from the crowded city. Externally, the early English tower and swept-up gables with obelisk pinnacles to the west front are unusual. Internally however, there have been a series of alterations but the Norman font and Jacobean woodwork have been retained. This church lost its parishioners

St. Philip and St. Jacob

when the neighbourhood was 'blitzed and houses demolished, but its story since then has been one of triumph over adversity. An active vicar has made it a centre for young people and action groups from outside the parish, and "Pip'n' Jay" is more alive today than it has ever been, a modern miracle.

Ahead of you is the Old Market underpass, a colossal £2½ million re-development scheme which swept away interesting, but badly damaged old eighteenth-century streets. The Bristol United Press Building on the right won an architectural award in 1974 and its purple brick and tile facings give a solidity to this corner. It is also the only place which will give you the correct time and the daily temperature.

Old Market Street was the site of the market for the castle garrison in the thirteenth century, and redeveloped in the seventeenth. Here, country people set up their stalls and markets and fairs were held regularly. The street itself is the widest thoroughfare in Bristol and until 1940, one of the busiest and most interesting. The Secretary of State has ruled that a conservation policy should be adopted for the whole street so that the future looks bright despite its present-day dilapidations.

The Stag and Hounds is a seventeenth-century inn with an eighteenth-century open colonnade, built on the site of the Court of Pie Poudre. This ancient court was a relic of Norman times for dealing summarily with market thieves and debtors. Justice was so swift that sentence was passed before the dust of the fair-ground was shaken off the malefactor's feet – hence "pied-poudre", meaning dusty feet. The need for such a court died when the markets ceased, but the court was ceremoniously opened on the last day of September until 1870, when the consumption of liquor, which was a prominent feature of the ceremony led to such riotous scenes that the affair was suppressed. However, until the recent reorganisation of the court system, a two-minute ceremony took place here on the last day of September when the court was formally proclaimed open, and then immediately adjourned.

It is here, in Old Market Street, that you can begin to see the devastation that can come when an area ceases to function as a living part of the city. The area of this walk, though not beautiful in the strict sense, does have its moments of beauty and provides an object lesson for the next generation. Everywhere you can see relics of a past which is in danger of dying completely. On the left, the King's cinema, Punch Bowl and Central Hall still stand but are due to be redeveloped when the economic situation improves. The next group, numbers 35–44 are "listed" seventeenth-century houses but they are deteriorating, visibly, by the minute, let alone the year. Number 44 was until 1960 an old "apothecary's" shop, with fascinating furniture, bottles and brass fittings. Fortunately, the contents are now in the city museum but the old shop is no more. The gateway leads into the re-built Steevens Almshouses, and the date 1686–1958 recalls the original foundation for 15 poor men by a philanthropic Alderman. In fact there are three almshouses in this street which are old foundations. Trinity Hospital North is now occupied by the Technical College but there is still the monument to its founder, John Barstaple to remind us that there has been an almshouse here since 1402. His wife, Isabella, in 1407 left money for a further almshouse for 28 women and this is now Trinity Hospital South on the other side of the road. The present building, is in Tudor style with fascinating external staircases, erected in 1867. Lower down, on this side of the street there is a group of well restored seventeenth- and eighteenth-century houses, now Inns, and the colonnaded front of Kingsley Hall, built 1706 as a meeting house.

As you turn left into Lawford Street note the only remaining pawnbroker's sign, in Bristol, three golden balls. In the bad old days pawnbrokers flourished in this area; now they are a rare sight. Redcross Street has been sacrificed to a car park, but one house, No. 7 has been lovingly restored with an eighteenth-century shell-hood. No. 6 is now an office block but a plaque recalls the fact that in a house on that site, Sir Thomas Lawrence was born in 1769. He was a child prodigy who became Royal Portrait painter to George III, and President of the Royal Academy. Redcross Lane is a narrow lane leading into a small court, typical of the crowded lanes, alleys of this area in the eighteenth and nineteenth centuries, which are no longer.

Lawford's Gate, now a road, was where a gate stood as one of the outer defences of the city until it was removed in 1769. It was at this gate that visiting royalty were received and welcomed by the mayor and his scarlet-robed brethren on the only passable route to Bath. The old gaol which once stood here was another victim of the 1831 Rioters' destructive vengeance. Colonel Fairfax attacked Lawford's Gate in 1645 and dashed down Old Market Street with a body of horsemen to capture the great gate of the castle from the Royalists. Lawford's Gate was a part of Bristol's history, now it is just a street leading into **Trinity Road**, which is also due for rebuilding. It is a pity that the 1868 Police Station and the 1829 Holy Trinity Church with its external twin turrets recalling King's

College, Cambridge, have to go. Such buildings become obsolete once people move away from the area. As you make your way down **Wade Street** and into **Newfoundland Road** you will see many pubs, standing alone, which once served thirsty workmen. Cross Newfoundland Road, into **St. Paul's Street** and you are entering an area built around 1789, for the wealthy, industrial class who wanted to live in the healthy countryside away from the

Portland Square

city. **Wilson Street** is virtually derelict, but No. 1 still stands. It was here, in a house which then had a walled garden and stabling for horses, that Elizabeth Blackwell, the first woman doctor in the world, lived with her family. Her father was a wealthy sugar-refiner who was frightened by the 1831 Riots and decided to start a new life in America. Elizabeth fought masculine prejudice and in 1849 qualified as a doctor, the first woman ever to do so. Wilson Street is also forever associated with George Muller who in 1836 opened his first orphanage at No. 6. Soon he took over Nos. 1, 2, 3, 4 and 14, but his orphans outgrew these houses and in 1849 he built the Ashley Down Muller's Orphanage for 2,000 waifs. It was his proud boast that he never asked for a penny, he just prayed and the Lord, and Bristolians, provided.

Portland Square was the first to be designed as an elegant and fashionable residential district around St. Paul's Church. For a century it flourished as a fashionable place of residence, with solid houses in Bath stone. No. 18, has a wrought-iron lamp-bracket and old door knocker and there are still some eighteenth century details left in the square despite so much insensitive development. The eighteenth century place name carved on the corner of Cave Street is still visible, boldly proclaiming **Portland Square**, and the

Surrey Lodge

central, oval garden, though overgrown is used by residents. St. Paul's Church, built 1794, received much ridicule when it was built as, "pagoda, wedding-cake architecture". It is odd, but it grows on you and enlivens this rather dull side.

Surrey Street leads into another square, **Brunswick Square**, built in 1769. Surrey Lodge is a tiny essay in Greek Doric style and was the lodge to Surrey House, now demolished. It is worth a visit as it is the entrance to the Unitarian Cemetary where there are some interesting old monuments, unusual in a city. The Square was much damaged in the 'blitz, but in its heyday it housed many notable Bristolians. The Congregational Chapel, built in 1834 is now a warehouse. Although the houses have deteriorated the frontages are to be retained and there are plans to revitalise the area. The cast-iron stone curbs are a unique feature of Bristol street-furniture and will be preserved. **Wilder Street** on the left has only one surviving house, but the original cobblestones and winding road lead to the elegant Full Moon Hotel, a superb example of a seventeenth-century coaching inn with eighteenth-century

King Square

additions. It was built to cater for the many visitors to the St. James Fair and has been in continuous use as an inn. The interior is spacious and has a fine Jacobean staircase to admire, while you have a lunchtime drink. St. James Fair has gone and the impressive new office block before you stretches for 250 yards spanning the main road. It does have a certain massive dignity, fronting modern stores.

So far, you have seen areas which over the years have lost much of their former glory, but now you can make your way up to the Kingsdown area which has been rescued from the same fate and is once again a highly desirable place of residence. Make your way across North Street to Dighton Street, making a short detour into **Charles Street** where No. 4 still stands. This is a typical mid-eighteenth-century middle class residence where Charles Wesley spent all his married life, 1749–1771. His two famous organist sons, Charles and Samuel, were born here and he himself worshipped and was buried in the nearby church of St. James. The only large house left in Dighton Street was once the home of the Harford family, noted Bristol bankers. **King Square** was developed on the southern slope of Kingsdown, in 1755, but has been sadly mutilated by alteration and bombing. No. 5 is the Arts Centre, where films and plays are presented in an informal atmosphere. It is worthwhile calling in and checking on performances which might interest you. No. 7 has a good porch and No. 12 some fine ironwork, but the interest of the Square is as a focal point for a series of streets and parallel terraces along the hillside, linked by narrow and steeply rising lanes. Spring Hill, with its cobbles and stepped pavements leads up to Kingsdown, the first planned suburb in Georgian Bristol. In the middle ages the down had been used as an exercise plain for the castle garrison and, in the Civil War of 1642, when new defences for the city had to be hastily constructed, the whole length of this down was linked by earth ramparts along the line of **Kingsdown Parade** to a fort at Montague Place and a larger fort at Windmill Hill, now the Royal Fort. By the eighteenth century these defences had been destroyed and the prosperous middle classes took their doctors' advice and turned to this salubrious area when building their new houses.

Walk along **Somerset Street** and admire the "street furniture" here; stone setts, bollards, old lamps, railings and traditional pennant footpaths which you will not find preserved anywhere else. The houses are all different and interesting but the view down Spring Hill over the city alone, is worth climbing up so far. **Kingsdown Parade** dates from about 1760 and the houses have a variety of steps, door-knockers, iron-work and doorways. Over the doorway of No. 29 is a plasterwork laurel wreath commemorating Wellington's victory over Napoleon. You can look back to the Royal Fort and forward to the heights of Ashley Down and remember that this was the site of the Civil War defences with forts and batteries commanding those two points, and where the fighting was at its bloodiest. The defence line continued along Freemantle Square and down Nine-Tree Hill into Stokes' Croft and you can walk this way too, remembering that although much has gone, enough has been retained to enable you to complete your picture of eighteenth-century Bristol.

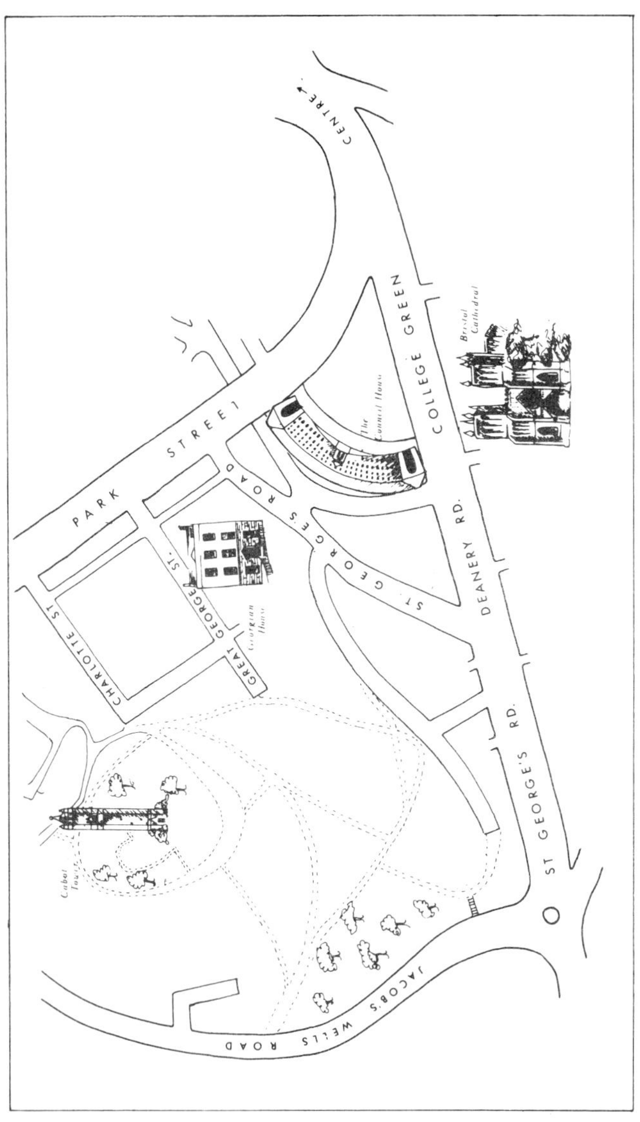
CENTRE
PARK STREET
COLLEGE GREEN
Bristol Cathedral
The Council House
ST GEORGE'S ROAD
DEANERY RD.
ST GEORGE'S RD.
CHARLOTTE ST
GREAT GEORGE ST.
Georgian House
Cabot Tower
JACOB'S WELLS ROAD

WALK 7

Bridgehead – College Green – Park Street – Great George Street – Brandon Hill – Jacob's Wells Road – Hotwell Road – Centre.

Here, at the Bridgehead, you are standing near the spot from which John Cabot and his son Sebastian sailed in the little ship Matthew with eighteen crewmen in 1497 to discover Newfoundland. Cabot's landfall on the coast of North America had been made possible by the financial backing of Bristol merchants and the navigational experience of Bristol sailors. His son, Sebastian, told many different versions about his life but he did say that he was born in Bristol and taken to Venice when he was four. He certainly spent some of his adult years here with his father, so we can claim him as a Bristolian. If you look up to your left you can see the Cabot Tower on the skyline at Brandon Hill and this walk will include a visit there. Before you leave the Bridgehead, look at the particularly suitable statue of Father Neptune watching over the city. The lead covered statue by Joseph Rendall was originally set up near old Bristol Bridge but came here in 1949. There are two other interesting plaques commemorating other events in Bristol's maritime history here at the Bridgehead.

As you turn left into College Green, spare a glance at the unusual 'E' Shed, a warehouse which will be preserved as part of the new Docks complex. **College Green** itself, a green 3 acre expanse in front of the new Council House, has been a popular spot for centuries. It is alleged by some writers that St. Augustine himself preached here in A.D. 596 introducing Christianity to Britain. Certainly, this open space has had a long connection with the church and the College of St. Augustine, now the Cathedral. On the left is the Royal Hotel, built 1868, incorporating two of the last remaining eighteenth-century houses which once surrounded this elegant green. We still have the statue of Queen Victoria, erected in 1887 to celebrate her Golden Jubilee but there are many Bristolians who regret the removal of the trees, railings and replica High Cross which once enhanced this scene. The building of the new Council House necessitated their removal.

On the south side of the Green is the Cathedral Church of the Holy and Undivided Trinity, founded in 1142 as the Abbey of St. Augustine (Black Canons) which in 1542, when all abbeys and monasteries were dissolved became the Cathedral. This Cathedral is a treasure house for the student of architecture, as successive centuries have contributed something that is either unique or in advance of its time. Little remains of the original Augustinian Abbey except the Norman Chapter House, the finest one in England; the Abbey Gatehouse and the archway to the Abbot's Lodging; and the night stairway to the Monks Dormitory, worn by continual use. You'll enjoy looking at the 28 misericords in the Choir Stalls exhibiting the grotesque humour of the medieval carver. There are some attractive monuments, including one to Sir John Young the founder of Wadham College, Oxford, with his wife Joan and their eight children in attendance. The Elder Lady Chapel has amusing figures in the spandrels of the arches and the whole chapel is a blaze of colour, the glory of the Middle Ages. These are the most attractive features of the Cathedral but the best way to get the most out of your visit is to buy the splendid coloured guide-book and explore the Cathedral in detail. Behind the Cathedral, through the Abbey Gateway, is the Cathedral School, founded by Henry VIII and once a Direct Grant School but now Independent.

The Central Library adjoins the Norman Abbey Gateway and though built in 1906 it fits in very well. Look up at the three panels of figures; the first is of Chaucer and six Canterbury pilgrims, the middle one of Caedmon and six saints and the last of a Minstrel and six Saxon writers. The Library of course is a storehouse of knowledge but try to find time to go in and ask to see the Bristol Room which is a replica of part of the Old King Street Library with its carved chimney piece attributed to Grinling Gibbons.

Now, cross over and take a closer look at the new Council House. This crescent-shaped building with its golden roof-top unicorns, the supporters of the city Arms, was opened by Queen Elizabeth in 1956 though the foundation stone had been laid in 1935 and the shell of the building was almost complete when the war broke out and all work ceased. Beneath the central archway is the symbolic figure of a Tudor sailor holding the charter from Henry VII, and from his waist hangs an astrolabe used for measuring the altitude of the sun or stars. The sculptor, Charles Wheeler, said the sailor was meant to be John Cabot. Go in through the main entrance door and facing you is a fine blue and gold clock, encircled by the signs of the Zodiac and having a wind indicator. If the City Council is in session you can go into the Public gallery and see how your city is governed. The Council Chamber is equipped in the style of the House of Commons and the ceiling is painted to show "Bristol at all times in its history". In the large Conference Hall, the names of Mayors and Lord Mayors with their dates of office are inscribed around the walls. In the Lord Mayor's Parlour the Civic Insignia, including the four Swords of State and maces, is displayed. Although the public is entitled to look around its Council House, it would be as well to contact the Commissionaire at the desk as he can be most helpful.

Behind the Council House in **St. George's Road** is a last group of three eighteenth-century houses reminding us of those in nearby College Street where Coleridge and Southey once lodged. To the right of this group is Brunel House with an imposing classical façade. Built in 1839 by Brunel as the Royal Western Hotel, it is a survivor of his dream of a transatlantic routeway and was intended to accommodate railway passengers from Temple Meads waiting for their ship, "The Great Western". Today it is used as offices but the façade is unaltered.

As you continue right towards Park Street you see on the corner, the Freemasons' Hall, built in 1821 by Sir Robert Cockerell as, "The Philosophic Institution for the Advancement of Science, Literature and the Arts". Under the semicircular portico is a friese, another example of the work of the Bristol sculptor, Edward Baily whose figure of Nelson tops the column in Trafalgar Square.

Now you are in **Park Street** itself. This was the first street to be built up the hill in Bullock's Park in 1762 and though it was severely blitzed, it has been rebuilt with great accuracy. There is one fine original house left, No. 51 with the original Georgian doorway and short, rail-lined steps which existed before the houses were adapted for shops. Park Street looks, and is, steep but we are going to branch off at No. 47 and leave the rest of

Gt. George Street Drawing Room

Park Street for another walk – coming down, not going up! No. 47 was one of the first shops to be converted from a private dwelling house and the railings have been lovingly preserved. It was here on the corner that Henry Cruger lived from 1757–1770. Cruger was born in America but came to Bristol, became Mayor and a Member of Parliament with Edmund Burke, finally returning to America where he became a Senator in New York State. There can't be many cities which can claim an American Senator among their ex-Mayors and M.P.'s or one who remained a British City Councillor until his death.

This corner house leads you into **Great George Street**, a

superb street with some fine houses built about 1780 by Thomas Paty and his sons to suit individual clients rather than for speculative building. The best of these houses is No. 7, now known as The Georgian House, one of the first and most finely preserved period museums of its kind. This house was originally built for John Pinney, a West India merchant who wanted to live in "an airy part of Bristol", with a superb view over the city and his ships moored in the harbour. The Pinneys were close friends of the poet Wordsworth and his sister and it is most probable that Wordsworth first met his fellow poets Coleridge and Southey at this house. Although there are six floors and a stable block, only three floors are on view but they give a good picture of the way in which a prosperous eighteenth-century merchant lived. All the main living rooms are at the back away from the noise of carriages, and the Drawing Room contains some of the best period furniture in the house. The most fascinating room is undoubtedly the kitchen in the basement where the eighteenth-century labour-saving devices seem horrifyingly laboursome to modern eyes. Another unique "mod-con" was the large stone plunge-bath in the basement, a huge walk-in bath about ten foot long and five foot wide. John Pinney wrote to a friend, "I now subscribe to a Cold Bath, and goes in every morning which I finds to be of great service to me". These West India merchants must have been a hardy lot. Entrance to the museum is free and a well-illustrated Guide Book can be obtained at the desk.

Across the road is St. George's chapel, built in 1823 as a parish church for this expanding area. The inhabitants must have had great stamina to climb up the imposing ascent of three flights of steps to the Doric porch. Another interesting group of houses is the Royal Colonnade on the right and No. 25 on the left is well-preserved and has a good iron-work lantern holder.

The green expanse before you is Brandon Hill, twenty nine acres of public park with a panoramic view of the city from the summit. Tradition says that St. Brendan had a chapel here in A.D. 577 *after* he had discovered America! Bristolians remain convinced that their challengers Brendan and Cabot should have shared Columbus's fame. Apart from St. Brendan other recluses and a poor hermit have lived up here in seclusion.

Bristol women have enjoyed the right to hang their washing on the south-west slopes from ancient times and in 1625 the Corporation acquired Brandon Hill "to keep it well prepared, maintaining the hedges and bushes and admitting the drying of clothes by towns-men and towns-women as had anciently been accustomed".

The Cabot Tower at the top of the hill was built in 1897 to commemorate the voyage from the port of Bristol of John

View From Brandon Hill

Cabot in 1497 and his discovery of America, under letters patent granted by King Henry VII to that navigator and his sons Sebastian, Lewis and Sanctus. This is an attractive tower built of red-sandstone in Venetian Gothic style. If you have chosen a fine day climb the 109 steps to the top and get the best, panoramic view of Bristol. You can, literally, see over the city as far as Dundry and count off the many landmarks, church spires, fine buildings, crescents and the river which you have come to know on these walks. At a lower level, walk around the tower and you will go past a signpost indicating the site of the chief Civil War defences during the 1643 and 1645 sieges. A part of the wall and the defensive earthworks have been retained and you can see how difficult it must have been for an attacker to force a way up and then over that rampart.

Another interesting notice declares, "No carpet beating allowed before 6 a.m. or after 9 a.m." The posts remain though the line on which carpets were once hung has gone, but if you

Queen Elizabeth's Hospital

feel you'd like to hump your carpet up here to be beaten, they would probably find you a piece of rope! If you walk down the hill on the far side you should come down the steps into **Jacob's Wells Road** by the side of the old Police Station dated 1836. This was one of the first to be set up in the provinces but it is now used as part of the VIth Form block for Queen Elizabeth's Hospital, the Tudor-style building to the right built in 1847. The school was originally founded in 1586 by John Carr as, "an hospital or place for bringing up of poor children and orphans, being men children whose parents are deceased, or fallen into decay and not able to relieve them", and started life in the Gaunts near St. Mark's Chapel, and later at St. Bartholomew's

Christmas Steps. Here however, in 1847 they moved to the purer air of the hill and built on the site of a 600 year old Jewish cemetery, whose gravestones having been used in the base of the building it has been wittily observed that, "The boys educated at the school will always have a good Hebrew foundation". The boarders of the school wear a uniform of dark blue cassocks and yellow stockings similar to that of Christ's Hospital and they add a touch of colour to the Clifton scene.

You can make your way down Jacob's Wells Road, passing the Bristol Carpet Cleaning Company, site of John Hippisley's Theatre which he built outside the city boundaries in 1729 but which was outdated by The Theatre Royal in King Street, to St. George's Road and back to the Centre, a short if uninteresting road.

WALK 8

Queen's Road – Park Place – Berkeley Square – Park Street – Unity Street – Orchard Street – College Green.

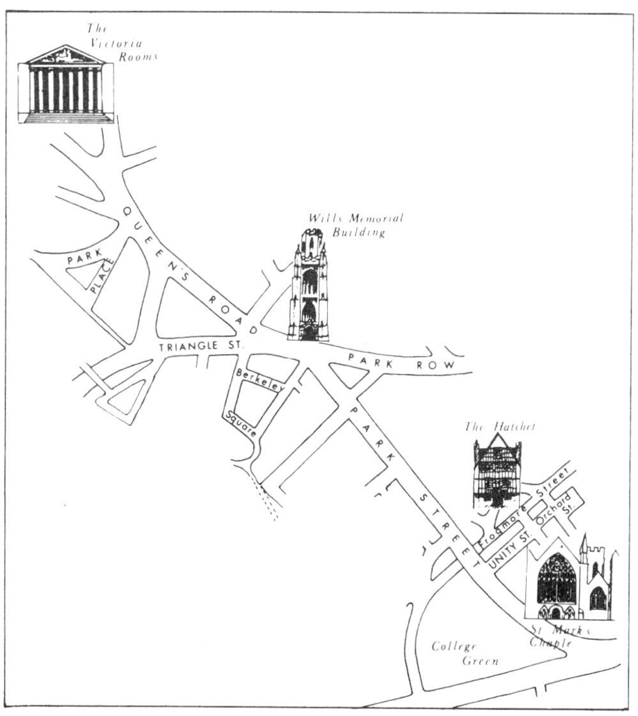

Queen's Road for many Bristolians is still "the" place in which to be seen on a morning's stroll or shopping expedition, despite the fact that in term time it is completely taken over by students. The Victoria Rooms stand at the head of Queen's Road and occupies the finest site in Clifton. The 1840 building, with well proportioned Corinthian columns and classic carvings reminiscent of a Greek temple, was originally built to serve the polite Clifton area with concerts and play-readings. It was here that Charles Dickens gave readings in 1866–1869 and Oscar Wilde's lectures on Aesthetics drew huge audiences. The Rooms now belong to the University and served as "The Union", that spiritual home of students, until a new, plusher one was built up the road in 1966. To the right of the Victoria Rooms is a small one-room building known as the "Studio" where the Bristol inventor of cinematography, Friese-Greene, opened his first photographic business in 1880. In front of the "Vic Rooms" is a superior statue of Edward VII in full Garter robes, set up in 1912 but perhaps a more interesting one is the memorial to the men of the Gloucester Regiment who fell in the Boer War. Have a look at the soldier stepping forward with fixed bayonet – some say that he is on the wrong foot and a disgrace to the regiment! Turn aside for a while, into **Park Place**, a quiet little back water, with flowering trees and green space, which has been tastefully restored as fine little town-houses with their original neat, shell-hoods. The large building is the old Pro-Cathedral built in 1850, so called because it was only to be in place of a Cathedral until such time as one could be erected. It had to serve until 1972 when the new concrete Roman Catholic Church of St. Peter and St. Paul was built in Pembroke Road, Clifton.

Queen's Road contains a fine range of uniform Victorian buildings once known as the Royal Promenade which today have been converted into shops below while still retaining the upper uniformity of style. Here there are department stores, bookshops and boutiques to lure you but save some of your time for the rest of the road and the City Museum and Art Gallery. These were once two separate buildings but only the façade of the Museum survived the blitz. It is the 1867 building to the right in free Venetian style like the Doge's Palace, now housing the University Refectory.

The City Museum and Art Gallery is open every week-day from 10 a.m. to 5.30 p.m. and your problem will be trying to see everything before it closes. The Museum lays special emphasis on local history and the exhibits and settings are outstanding. Apart from the fixed displays there are regular visiting collections and special exhibits. The children really won't want to leave this place with its bookstall and souvenir shop in the main hall, and Dinosaur snack-bar.

Outside, on the wall, is a plaque indicating that "from this place, July 26th 1643 Colonel Henry Washington attacked the parliamentary defences between Royal Fort and Brandon Hill. With a small force he effected Washington's Breach, through which Royalist troops entered Bristol and compelled its capitulation". This Colonel was a collateral ancestor of the President, George Washington and so here is another Bristol–America link.

The Wills Memorial Building of the University of Bristol completes this trio of fine buildings. The 1925 tower, in perpendicular Gothic style, is 215 feet high. If you are near the tower at the hour you will hear Great George the most musical ten-ton, E flat bell in Europe strike the hour in fine style. You can go into the entrance hall of the University and see the fan-vaulting, then go up the steps into the Great Hall which has been restored after the blitz had gutted it.

Cross over this busy road using the pedestrian crossing to your right and make a detour into Berkeley Square. This Square was another of those speculative buildings which bankrupted its original contractor when the French war of 1793 caused financial panic. The houses were finished very handsomely and this became a fashionable address. At No. 7 was born John Addington Symonds the Victorian critic who wrote perceptively about the Italian Renaissance and indeed died in Rome. John Loudon McAdam lived at No. 23 when he was General Surveyor of roads belonging to the Bristol Turnpike Trust. He made Bristol roads a pattern for the whole world when he invented a new method of road construction and gave a new word to the language, "macadamised". The original Civic High Cross had been given away to grace Henry Hoare's new estate at Stourhead and in 1850 a replica was set up in College Green only to be taken down in its turn and left to deteriorate. Fortunately, a group of civic-minded citizens managed to save the top half of the cross, and now, restored, it rests in the gardens of Berkeley Square.

Back in **Park Street** again, you have a fine view over the city and can imagine Colonel Washington's men charging down

High Cross, Berkeley Square

the hill to take the Cathedral and College Green from the Parliamentarians. You won't charge down – it's too steep and there are too many bookshops to distract you, but once at the bottom turn into Unity Street and on to **Orchard Street**. This, another quiet backwater, was built in 1717 in the orchard of the

Gaunts' Hospital which once stood here. It is the earliest group of domestic buildings retained in their original condition which the city has, and there are some excellent examples of Georgian railings, door-furniture, foot-scrapers. The group numbers 27, 28 and 29 is exceptionally fine with mask keystones and original door-knockers.

Orchard Street

Denmark Street leads into Frogmore Street and The Hatchet Inn, once part of a row of seventeenth-century half-timbered houses and though dated 1606, it goes back to the sixteenth century. The Inn has many sporting connections especially with pugilists like Tom Cribb and Jem Mace and was one of the last inns to have a cock fighting pit as an attraction. The Hatchet is now isolated on an island but adds dignity to the rather undignified, loud, modern Entertainment Centre behind it. Continue up Unity Street and you reach College Green once more with St. Mark's Chapel on the left. The whole of this area has names which are connected with the original Gaunts' Hospital; Orchard Street, Frogmore Street where the fishponds were situated, Culver Street, the site of the dovecotes, and now the Chapel of the Gaunts which is the only building left of the medieval hospital for the relief of the poor, founded in 1220 by Maurice de Gaunt. After the dissolution of the monasteries the property was bought, not by an individual, but by the Corporation of Bristol, and thus it came about that Bristol is the only

St. Mark's Chapel

city in the kingdom to have a civic chapel for the exclusive use of the Corporation. St. Mark's is also known as The Lord Mayor's Chapel and is open every day except Friday. It's a beautiful chapel and gives a good idea of what the church of a smaller, religious house was like. The entrance is down a flight of steps so that the whole church is virtually seen at once, spread out below. There really are so many gems here that it is difficult to know what to look at first. The chapel is well lit and the fifteenth- and sixteenth-century stained glass catches your eye as does the black and gold roof of the nave. The side chapel is the Poyntz chantry and contains fascinating monuments, some highly coloured, but all giving an accurate picture of the fashions of four centuries. Children will be interested in the monument to John Cookin who died 1627 at the age of eleven and is presented in the smart costume of the time of Charles I with his pens, ink-horn and books behind him. Though small,

College Green

this is a most complete chapel and you will be really charmed by its treasures. At the side of the chapel is a little archway which leads to the little known side and rear view of the tower built in 1487.

Your walk finishes on College Green, where if it is fine you can join the many Bristolians who sit on this open space enjoying the view across to the Cathedral or up to the University and even, perhaps, find time to eat a lunchtime sandwich.

WALK 9

Clifton Down – Sion Hill – Caledonia Place – Cornwallis Crescent – Windsor Terrace – Dowry Square – The Hotwells.

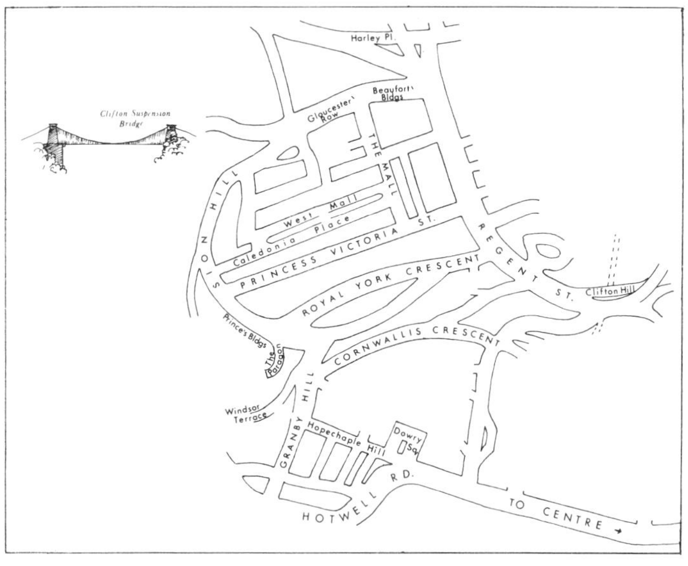

The total area of Clifton and Durdham Downs is 442 acres, but don't worry, you are not going to try to walk it all in one go! Make the extreme southern point of the Clifton Downs the start of this Walk which will give you a taste of life in eighteenth-century Bristol during its heyday as part of The Hotwell Spa scene. This oasis of green was a popular spot in the

1790's. Harley Place on your left is a fine row of balconied Georgian houses and one small house, Penrose Cottage, was the home of the poet Walter Savage Landor. "I have a great love for Clifton above all places in England", he wrote to his fellow poet, Southey, in 1838. Litfield Place, originally lead-field, reminds us that the Downs were mined, quarried and dug since Roman times and there is an interesting item in Clifton Parish Church Register for 1574, "Dick Dunstan and John Langton being myners of Mendippe did mine and dig for lyme and lead upon the Downs and being stifled with smoake, dyed and were buried". The Merchant Venturers bought up the whole area at the end of the nineteenth century to preserve it for future generations to enjoy.

Christ Church, built 1844, is a good parish church and has some interesting monuments of its own, and from St. Andrew's which was blitzed. Cross over Clifton Down Road and look at the obelisk and monument which came from Manilla Hall (now Manilla Road) where General Sir William Draper, a native of Bristol, lived in 1767. He erected this cenotaph to the memory of the officers and men of his regiment who fell at the capture of Manilla from the Spaniards in 1763, and one of the plaques records this "that future generations may know humanity is the characteristic of the British soldier". The obelisk is in honour of his hero, William Pitt, Earl of Chatham, and when Manilla Hall was demolished these monuments were rescued from the garden. Before you turn left into Sion Hill, pause to admire the Observatory and the Suspension Bridge briefly as you can examine them in more detail in your next walk. On this one you will look at the history of Clifton-on-the-Hill with its terraces and crescents to accommodate fashionable visitors. Although, historically, the building of Clifton-on-the-Hill began at the bottom of the spur of land which slopes sharply down to Hotwells and the Avon and worked its way up through a series of crescents and terraces to the relatively level terrain near the Downs, you will find it easier to start at the top and pace yourself on this slightly longer walk.

Sion Hill was begun in 1784, the year of the mania for speculative building; fortunately, this Hill itself is very attractive and has a variety of styles with the bow windows and iron-wrought verandahs mostly unchanged. This was a very popular place to stay with its fine view over a limestone gorge, unique in a city.

Before you turn left into Caledonia Place, have a look at St. Vincent's Priory. This is a fascinating Gothic-revival house dating from the beginning of the nineteenth century. Legend has it that it was built over caves which were once a Christian sanctuary. In fact, George Melhuish, the artist owner, discovered under some flagstones in the basement, a mysterious flight of stone steps leading to a cellar-like room with a bricked up door. The Priory façade is amusing with its stone caryatid figures and sphinxes but the house itself is only open to the public on special occasions.

Caledonia Place, though begun in 1843 is really Georgian in spirit. It is the south block of **The Mall** and forms an impressive terrace built on ground that slopes gently down from east to west so that the stepping down of each house front is slight. There are some verandahs at first floor level with Georgian balcony-railings, while the mounting blocks between the pavement and the roadway recall the days of landaus and broughams. A plaque on No. 16 recalls Lord Macaulay's stay here in 1852 when his mother ran a girls' school in Park Street. The north block is **West Mall** built in a similar style. Some of the houses retain their original knockers and door "furniture" – No. 24 has a pair of harps as footscraper and No. 34 a pair of hawks.

In 1806 "a meeting of the nobility and gentry of Clifton took place, for the purpose of considering a proposal for building a New Assembly Room, with Card Rooms etc.", and the result was the Clifton Assembly Rooms and Hotel in **The Mall**, directly opposite the entrance to West Mall. The architect was Francis Greenway, who will be mentioned later, but like a number of the Clifton speculative builders he went bankrupt and another businessman had to finish the Rooms. At the height of Clifton's popularity it was really a fine building with, "sets of apartments, drawing rooms, a coffee room; a shop for pastry and confectionery with an adjoining room for soups, fruit, and ices; hot, cold and vapour baths". It certainly had everything. In 1830 the future Queen Victoria was taken on a royal tour by her mother, the Duchess of Kent, and it was from the balcony of this Hotel that the ten year old Princess Victoria waved for the first time to the Bristol public. The Assembly Rooms inevitably became outmoded and in 1855 were converted into houses and shops. Today the Clifton Antiques Market occupies one wing and in itself is an added attraction with a market and good coffee bar.

Clifton Assembly Rooms

Princess Victoria Street itself is a sad mixture of shop fronts but behind it, Caledonia Mews has been competently converted into small dwelling houses. At the end of Princess Victoria Street is **Prince's Buildings**, originally Prince of Wales Crescent, 1796 with the Prince Regent's feathers, motto "Ich

Dien" and St. George and the dragon still carved on the pediment to remind us. Again many notable people stayed here, including Maria Edgeworth at No. 14 and the poet George Crabbe at No. 4 during the 1831 Riots. To the left of the buildings is **The Paragon**, built 1809 with interesting curved entrance porches and handsome brass knockers.

The flight of steps opposite leads you to Royal York Crescent the longest crescent in Europe, a quarter of a mile in

Royal York Crescent

length, and the highest and finest. All the front doors give onto this causeway and originally it was defended by a beadle. Today you can walk along this crescent unmolested and look across to Dundry and the hills of Somerset and admire the same view that the Empress Eugenie of France saw when she spent her happy schooldays here at No. 2. The Crescent was begun in 1790 and it was a most spectacular and expensive undertaking with a fortune spent in erecting the deep substructure of vaults and basements required to raise the terrace walk. The original builders became bankrupt in 1793 and then came the French

Revolutionary war which put a halt to speculative building in Clifton. The government intended to buy up the land for barracks, but this so alarmed the residents of Clifton that money was somehow raised to finish the Crescent. Now, its balconies and tent-shaped verandahs are the finest display of early nineteenth-century ironwork in Bristol.

Regent Street leads into **Clifton Hill** where the earliest mansions were built for individual wealthy families on the healthy hill overlooking the city. In this area, almost without exception, each house contains some details of interest, as all are well designed and beautifully enriched. It is up to you to pick out your favourites, but don't miss Clifton Court, now the Chesterfield Nursing Home built by William Halfpenny in 1742, though the earliest house, built in 1711, is further along, beyond the church gateway, where the Bishop of Bristol has his palace. The gateway leads to the blitzed site of St. Andrew's parish church, but the churchyard and delightful walk of pleached limes remain from late eighteenth century. It was from this spot that Prince Rupert surveyed the defences of Brandon Hill before making his assault on the city and thought it a good place to set up his batteries. The University now own Clifton Hill House on the left and Goldney House directly opposite but on certain days they are open to the public. Goldney House is especially interesting. The Quaker grocer, Thomas Goldney, made a great deal of money by investing in privateering ventures and built this house in 1720 with an orangery, canal, Gothic tower, bastions and underground shell grotto. All these unique features are behind the high wall and should be seen if at all possible.

Goldney Avenue at the side leads into **Cornwallis Crescent**, one of the most ambitious schemes during the height of speculative building, and a conscious effort to reproduce the splendours of the crescents at Bath. Once again the same story is repeated, the first builders went bankrupt in 1793. The architect, Francis Greenway took over one of the half-finished houses and became bankrupt himself. He then forged a contract concerning No. 34 and though sentenced to death, this was later changed to transportation to Australia. There he became one of Australia's best known architects and his portrait is depicted on their latest banknotes. The large house on the right, Cornwallis House, is now La Retraite High School.

At the end of Cornwallis Crescent, cross Granby Hill and go into **Windsor Terrace**. This is another of those early terraces but the interest lies in the farthest house known as Watt's Folly. It was William Watt who invented a method of making lead shot in his Old Shot Tower near St. Mary Redcliffe and made himself a fortune. He decided to build a house to suit his new

Windsor Terrace

status but the end house built on a succession of rubble-faced cellars down the side of the cliff cost so much to prop up that he became bankrupt and the terrace was finished by someone else in the Palladian manner. There is a superb view from here over the Avon. As you leave the terrace look up to your left and at the dramatic rear view of the Paragon.

It's downhill now all the way to the Hotwells. **Granby Hill** has a variety of decayed and restored houses of which the best, Rutland House, is typical of the larger lodging houses built for the Spa visitors. **Hope Chapel Hill** contains Hope Chapel itself built in 1786 as a Congregational chapel at the expense of Lady Henrietta Hope for her friends. This chapel was due for demolition but it has been saved as part of the job creation scheme and a new use will be found for it as a community centre for this revived part of old Bristol. Albemarle Row and Hope Square in the immediate vicinity have already been given a face-lift and are about to regain some of their former glory.

The chief residential area for the Hotwells Spa was **Dowry Square** at the bottom of the hill. The square was begun in 1717 and soon occupied by invalids and fashionable visitors. No. 2 has "Mr. Robert Young, Surgeon" inscribed over the door and No. 6 is a house full of associations. It was here that Dr. Beddoes in 1798 set up his Medical Pneumatic Institution, "for the benefit of the wealthy as well as of the indigent". He was convinced that air, modified in some form was essential for the successful treatment of T.B. and when he heard that, "a lady had her distressing symptoms all removed, from living the winter in a room with four cows", he thought he had found the cure. Clifton landladies however complained that, "they had not furnished their rooms for cattle", so Beddoes continued his experiments here with the aid of his nineteen year old Medical Superintendent, Humphrey Davy. Here Davy's experiments with nitrous oxide, "laughing gas", were carried out and men like Coleridge, Southey and The Wedgewood brothers tried the new sensation. Dr. Beddoes also had another future celebrity working for him as a physician, Peter Roget, who later completed the still-used Roget's "Thesaurus". At No. 9, the Reverend R. H. Barham, author of the "Ingoldsby Legends" stayed when ill and in fact, wrote his last poems here.

In Dowry **Parade** opposite the square, were the Assembly Rooms, now destroyed. We can imagine the activity which this area saw at the height of the Hotwells' season from this note by Dr. Sutherland who published a work on the spa water ... "There are lodgings near the Wells, convenient for such as are real invalids", but also, "there are Balls twice a week and card-playing every night". If the spa water didn't cure you at least your last days were one round of gaiety.

If you continue round the Hotwell Road to your right, you will come to the river Avon and the Gorge and it was here that the original hot springs flowed out of the cliff face and the visit of Charles II's wife, Catherine of Braganza in 1695 set the seal of approval on its healing qualities. A Pump Room was built on a projecting piece of land and the spa was in business. The Colonnade, a crescent of shops was built in 1780 to allow visitors to shop in comfort, but by that time Clifton-on-the-Hill had developed and offered greater attractions and the spa

Dowry Square

dwindled. The small colonnade with a portico is all that is left of this one-time big business venture. One of the contributory causes was the exhorbitant rents charged by the landladies and when it was realised that, though jolly enough, most of the visitors died despite the medicinal spring water, the Spa's days were at an end.

Your walk too is at an end and you can either walk up the zig-zag path to Clifton Down, or walk the length of the Hotwell Road back to the city centre.

WALK 10

Suspension Bridge – Clifton Down – Clifton College – The Zoo – The Sea Walls – Blackboy Hill.

"My first child, my darling, is actually going on glorious!" wrote an excited Isambard Kingdom Brunel in 1836, and he was, of course, referring to that ninth wonder of the world, the

Suspension Bridge

Clifton Suspension Bridge. It is not surprising that Brunel was excited about his "darling", as he had come to Bristol to recuperate, entered an open competition to design a bridge across the Avon and won, beating such master engineers as the

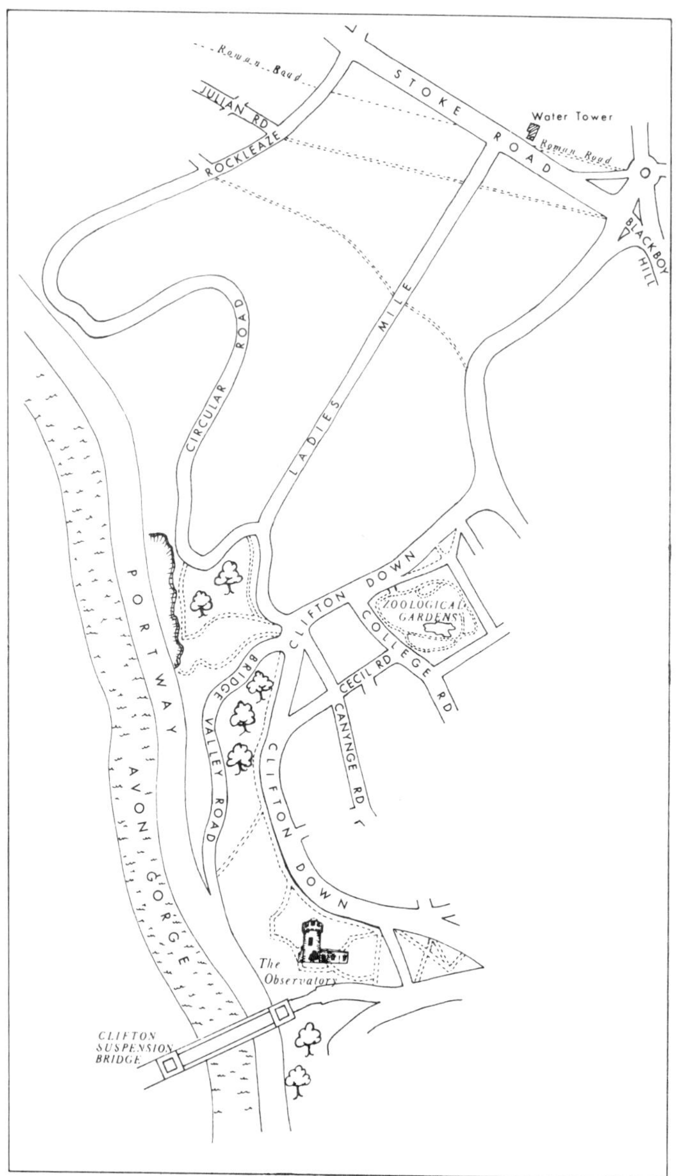
Roman Road
JULIAN RD
ROCKLEAZE
STOKE ROAD
Water Tower
Roman Road
BLACKBOY HILL
CIRCULAR ROAD
LADIES MILE
PORTWAY
CLIFTON DOWN
ZOOLOGICAL GARDENS
COLLEGE RD
CECIL RD
BRIDGE VALLEY ROAD
CANYNGE RD
CLIFTON DOWN
AVON GORGE
The Observatory
CLIFTON SUSPENSION BRIDGE

great Thomas Telford. However, the original money subscribed for the Bridge ran out in 1843 and work was abandoned for over twenty years until the chains from the Hungerford Bridge became available and the Suspension Bridge was finally completed. Here it is then, 702 ft. from pier to pier and 287 ft. above low water. Before the chains were thrown across, an iron bar had connected the two piers and passengers were hauled

The Observatory

across in a cradle, but you can do it the easy way – buy a 4p ticket and walk across. It is quite an experience from this height to look down on the Avon and enjoy the superb views over Bristol. It is sad to think that Brunel himself never walked across his bridge as he died two years before it was completed; thirty years after his design had been accepted. There is no monument or statue to him in Bristol, but this bridge is all the memorial he needs.

The **Observatory** on your left was originally a Snuff Mill which was burnt down in 1777 and rebuilt as a tower and Observatory by William West in 1829. One of its interesting features is the Camera Obscura which he put upon the summit of the tower and the old notice board which he proudly put outside is still displayed announcing, "The Camera Obscura to those unacquainted with it has a magical effect. The movement of persons, animals and carriages, the waving of foliage and the coming and going of ships being brought into the picture with distinction and vivid colouring of nature and affording a high gratification to the observer from the continual changes, varying effects of light and shade upon the landscape". He also excavated a tunnel to Ghyston's Cave, an opening in the rocks, once a hermitage which was only accessible from the face of the cliff. It is an eerie experience looking out over the river from this cave. This is the only camera obscura open to the public in Britain and you can use it from April to October when the view is at its best.

Around this observatory hill lie the remains of an Ancient British encampment and parts of the triple ramparts which protected the camp can be traced if you have the time and a little knowledge of what you are looking for. Once up here you can visualise why our ancestors chose this site at the head of the Avon Gorge for their secure camp.

Once you leave the observatory you can either walk along **Clifton Down Road** or keep to the grass and paths alongside. There are some fine, detached, Victorian houses in this road, and the last one with its entrance in Canynge Road, is the Mansion House. If the flag is flying then the Lord Mayor of Bristol is in residence at this particular mansion house, given to the city in 1874 by Alderman Procter to replace the one in Queen Square destroyed in the riots. On the first Wednesday of each month from 3–5 p.m., the Lady Mayoress is at Home to the people of Bristol, and you can call in at that time, see the magnificent Civic Plate and have a cup of tea with your chief citizens. There is one especially interesting piece of plate on display, the sixteenth-century silver salver which was stolen during the riots, cut into 167 pieces by the thief and sold. Later, the pieces were rescued and riveted together and the thief, James Ives sentenced to fourteen years transportation. When he had served his sentence he returned and had the nerve to ask to see the mended salver. It says much for the Bristolians' forgiving nature that he was allowed to.

If you go down Cecil Road and turn right into **College**

Road you come to the "campus" of Clifton College. The original Big Hall was designed by C. Hansom (his brother was responsible for the Hansom cabs) in 1862. The large playing fields are guarded by the statue of Earl Haig, an old boy of the school. Beyond the wooden games pavilion you can see in the distance, the modern tower of the Roman Catholic Cathedral of St. Peter and Paul, a new landmark on the Clifton skyline.

The Mansion House

Now, turn back along College Road to the Zoo, whose main entrance is on the Clifton Down itself. The correct name is the Zoological Gardens and indeed the gardens themselves are magnificent at all times of the year. The Zoo is open all the year round and is a treat for young and old with its unique white tiger family and the only pair of okapis in Britain. When you come out of the Zoo, be thankful that you are going to turn left along Clifton Down and not right, as this particular area was originally Gallows Acre Lane where the gibbet used to stand. Some grim events undoubtedly took place here and legend has it that the ghost of one Jenkins Prothero, the last criminal to be hanged in chains on the Downs in 1782, walks this haunted spot.

The pretty fountain at the top of Bridge Valley Road was donated by Alderman Procter in 1872, "to record the liberal gift of certain rights on Clifton Down made to the citizens by the Society of Merchant Venturers", and stands where the old tollgate of the Clifton Turnpike Road once stood. You can either follow the circular road or walk on the footpaths which

Sea Walls to Avonmouth

skirt the road and disappear into little thickets and dells. If you have children with you, your progress will be slow from now on, as there are so many exciting little glades overlooking the Avon, but do try to get to the Sea Walls, about half a mile along, as it is from here that you can obtain your best views over the Bristol Channel and to the Welsh Hills. The Avon Gorge is most dramatic and unique in a large city. To your left the Suspension Bridge spans the river as it flows on ultimately past the Horseshoe Bend and Pill to Avonmouth.

There are many notices here indicating that the rocks are in a dangerous condition and on no account should you ignore these warnings. You can see all you need from this Sea Wall, which a generous citizen, John Wallis built in 1746 at this vantage point. The Portway below you is five miles long and 300 foot down – it's a long way to fall. In summer this is a favourite spot to relax and have an ice-cream or even a drink from a nearby water fountain with a little bowl for dogs below it. Continue along **Rockleaze** and then near Julian Road cut across the Downs by the path where the old Roman road used to run. This was the straight road taken by the Romans as they made their way from Bath to their embarkation port for Wales at Sea Mills (Abonae). Julian Road itself is the old Via Julia and it leads straight to the old harbour. Today however, the area has been so built up that you cannot take the same road and in any case you will do better to make your way across the Downs to the Water Tower remembering that this is an area which saw Prince Rupert leading his defeated army out of Bristol in 1645; the early non-Conformists holding their open air services in 1670; horse-racing and highwaymen in the eighteenth century, and quarrying and mining until 1861 when the Merchant Venturers finally bought this land and gave it to Bristolians, and visitors, to enjoy for ever.

This has been a long, healthy walk so you can catch a bus from the Blackboy Hill to the Centre or back to the Suspension Bridge without feeling guilty.

SOME OUTSTANDING EVENTS IN BRISTOL'S HISTORY

1086 – Domesday Book records that Bristol is part of the Manor of Barton.
1170 – Bristol Castle built by Robert, Earl of Gloucester.
1148 – St. Augustine's Abbey founded – later to become the Cathedral.
1216 – First Mayor of Bristol appointed.
1220 – Gaunts' Hospital founded.
1239 – River Frome diverted and new channel cut.
1373 – Bristol created a County by Edward III.
1442 – St. Mary Redcliffe rebuilt by William Canynges.
1497 – John Cabot sailed in ship, "Matthew" and discovered Newfoundland.
1532 – Robert and Nicholas Thorne founded the Grammar School.
1542 – Henry VIII creates Diocese of Bristol.
1574 – Elizabeth I visited Bristol.
1586 – John Carr founded Queen Elizabeth's Hospital.
1613 – First free Library established.
1636 – Edward Colston born.
1642 – Civil War began.
1643–1645 – Bristol held by Royalists.
1654 – Bristol Castle destroyed.
1655 – First Quaker Meeting held.
1681 – William Penn established Quaker colony in Pennsylvania.
1702 – Queen Square begun.
1737 – Bristol Royal Infirmary opened.
1739 – John Wesley opens his New Room in the Horsefair.
1743 – The Exchange built by John Wood in Corn Street.
1766 – The Theatre Royal opened.
1768 – Bristol Bridge rebuilt.
1780 – Clifton on the hill developed.
1831 – Reform Riots in which Mansion House, Customs House and part of Queen Square destroyed.
1836 – Zoological Gardens opened.
1841 – The Great Western Railway opened between Bristol and London.
1843 – The "Great Britain" built by Brunel, launched by Prince Albert.
1862 – Clifton College opened.
1864 – Clifton Suspension bridge completed.
1876 – University College founded.
1899 – Queen Victoria grants Bristol a Lord Mayoralty.
1926 – Portway opened between Bristol and Avonmouth.
1956 – New Council House opened by Queen Elizabeth II.